"There are certain times in busii
info, or even privileged info, what you need is a great wizard to swoop in
and make it all better. Troy Broussard is such a wizard when it comes to
Infusionsoft.

Beyond his head-spinning tech skills, Troy totally "gets it" when it comes
to working with us creative types who quickly develop (*and often, cause*)
headaches when we encounter deep tech. I'm thrilled that he wrote this
book because it helps even tech-averse daydreamers like me understand
how to get the most out of my CRM.

I'm even more thrilled that I can skip reading it and just hire Troy. At
least for now, while I can still afford him."

Kevin Rogers, Founder, CopyChief.com

"Troy Broussard is an Infusionsoft genius! He showed us capabilities we
had no idea existed. Read this book, and if you ever have a chance to
learn from him in person, take it!"

Bill Harris, Founder & CEO, Centerpointe Research Institute

"If you are using Infusionsoft in your business you MUST read Troy's
book. You will discover numerous ways to scale your business, make
more money and save time. Plus, as a byproduct, your employees will be
smiling.

You see Troy is a rare breed, he can effectively communicate with the
best of marketers as well as the non-verbal techies. Frankly there is no
one better when it comes to Infusionsoft. He is truly the Master!"

**MaryEllen Tribby, #1 Best Selling Author, Reinventing the
Entrepreneur: Turning Your Dream Business Into Reality
CEO, Met Edge Media**

"Troy Broussard is truly a one of a kind treasure that business owners dream of crossing paths with. An elite marketing mind, incredible communication skills, plus world class technical know-how of highly sophisticated software and tools, gives Troy the capability to turn your marketing dreams into a reality.

He goes where others in his field would never dare, nor would they believe what he's capable of doing is even possible. Do yourself and your business results a favor, and tap into all that you can of Troy's wisdom, products and services."

Tom Beal, CEO of RemarkableMarketing.com

"I had a successful business that generated all of its sales online. I had all the old school basic elements in place. Troy took my business and updated not only the look and feel of the site but how effectively we deal with customers from initial contact through marketing and customer service.

Infusionsoft like Photoshop can seem expansive and be a bit daunting. Troy helped pull it all together by not only setting it up but teaching us how to maintain, manage and get the most out of it. I'm confident Troy has helped us build the foundation necessary to take my business to the next level and beyond and look professional doing it."

Dennis Linkletter, KomodoKamado.com

"Massive thanks to Troy Broussard who clarified exactly how to track ROI ad spend through Infusionsoft in a way I've never seen done before. I highly recommend Troy for anyone who uses Infusionsoft and wants clear and actionable conversion tracking - definitely the guy to call when it comes to making Infusionsoft really work for your funnels..."

Naomi Kuttner, Solo-Entrepreneur, New Zealand

"Troy is one of those 'crazy types' that pushes the limits of Infusionsoft beyond what even IS thought was possible. It is very much worth your time to check out what they do – and if you ever have an unsolvable issue, it's likely they can solve it for you..."

Will Mitchell, Co-Founder, StartupBros.com, Tampa Bay, Florida

"I am not very easily impressed, but can confidently say that Troy is truly an expert in the field. During my one-on-one mentoring calls with Troy, I am left with complete satisfaction and an awareness that "this guy knows what he is talking about." He is very clear, has impeccable "best business" practices, and is generous with his information. I wish I found him when I first started using Infusionsoft. His methods and logic are awesome!"

Kc Rossi, bigtreehealing.com

"Can I just do another huge Thank You to Troy Broussard and his team - they really have an amazing knowledge of Infusionsoft. We have been having an issue that Infusionsoft customer support has been completely confused by - yet they came up with two potential solutions for us in just 10 minutes! Much, much appreciated!"

Heloise Laight, Canonbury Publishing, UK

"I don't know where I'd be without Troy's coaching and support. I've been an infusion user for 5 years and after working with Troy and his software, I've been able to take my business and automated systems to a new level. One that takes so much more stress off my shoulders. What I find most helpful besides that, though, is that Troy understands business and can guide me on the steps I need to take in order to get the results I want as fast as possible. It is a double value having a coach / mentor who also knows more about Infusionsoft then their own support teams!"

Nick Fosburg, Founder, BarMarketingSuccess.com

"We run dozens of Infusionsoft accounts for 6, 7 and 8-figure clients and the knowledge of these guys is an absolute game changer - and has already saved me so much time, improved attendance for our webinars, boosted conversions and helped us segment our campaigns even further. We've also moved all of our clients over to their software and not only saved a TON of money, but have enjoyed the UI and speedy response of the team anytime I've needed anything as well."

Taylor Welch, Advanced Funnel & Infusionsoft Specialist

"I've been working with John and Troy for nearly a year now and can't recommend them strongly enough. Beyond just their technical Infusionsoft expertise, I rely on them for their strategic marketing advice. In a recent launch I ran with their assistance, I exceeded my entire launch goal in just the first 24 hours and blew away my intended sales goal by 523% over what I thought it would yield! I recommend you do what I did and hire these guys before they get too booked up..."

Frank Rumbauskas,
NY Times Best Selling Author, Never Cold Call

"I love the power of MyFusion Helper (from Troy's other company). Troy and his team are first class when it comes to customer service and their knowledge of Infusionsoft. Troy also leads the local Infusionsoft User Group (here in Orlando) that I attend."

Christopher Yates, Photographer, Orlando, Florida

"Troy is a true marketing and automation Ninja! His advice and guidance give me the ability to maximize my investment in Infusionsoft to grow my business."

Rachel Wall, RDH, BS, Founder of InspiredHygiene.com

FOREWORD

If you want to run a business that's built for scale, automation is key. It is what makes the difference between running a business where you're trying to juggle dozens of plates in the air, and a business that generates passive income, giving you the financial and time freedom you want.

And today, automation is more important than ever before, because of the advanced segmentation that is happening in the market. It used to be, when you set up a sales funnel, everyone saw the same ads, the same landing page, and the same sales page. But now it is possible to customize and segment your audience, and then deliver different sales messages and sequences based on the needs of your customers.

One of the most common questions I received after publishing my #1 best-selling book, Ask, was "how do you actually execute some of the automation elements of the Ask Method?" If you're not familiar with the Ask Method, it is a way to find out what your customers really want (and give it to them) using the power of surveys and quizzes in an automated way. The Ask Method uses a quiz to segment customers into one of several categories, called "buckets," in order to customize the marketing messages that they receive.

And while the book Ask describes the methodology for doing this, I wasn't able to cover some of the more advanced automation tactics in the book. For example, when you're asking a series of questions in your quiz, how do you add those data points to someone's contact record in Infusionsoft? That's just one of the questions that comes up when people get into the nitty gritty details of executing the Ask Method, and it is something that I was unable to cover in depth in the book.

That's where Troy Broussard comes in, and that's why you're reading this book. Troy is a leader in automation marketing, especially in Infusionsoft. In the online mastermind community that I run, I've seen the support that he's given our community members, going above and beyond the call of duty to support them. For example, one of our members came to Troy with a problem that had even the Infusionsoft support team stumped, and Troy came up with two possible solutions in just ten minutes.

He got on the phone with a member to explain to them how to track ROI on ad spend through Infusionsoft in a way that they'd never heard of before.

He's shared advanced tactics and tools that I haven't seen shared anywhere else, regularly posting his insights in the group on things like how to split test to a large list of 10K or more using Infusionsoft, and other advanced Infusionsoft hacks.

I was so impressed with his contributions to the community and his knowledge that I invited Troy to do a guest expert call for the group on the topic of automation, and Troy went above and beyond the call of duty to not only deliver a valuable presentation, but to answer members' questions in detail.

Troy's software, MyFusion Helper, is a big hit in our community as well. Members have told me that they're running dozens of Infusionsoft apps and Troy's software is essential to their business. His name is the one that gets mentioned when there's an Infusionsoft question, and he always rises to the challenge with valuable advice and tips.

And while I only use Infusionsoft for part of my business, the advantages that it gives us in terms of automation have had a huge impact on the business. There's no question that marketing automation has transformed the way we think about online sales. And that's especially true when it comes to the Ask Method...this method would not exist if it wasn't for the tools that allow us to automate, including quizzes that 23,000 people take every single day.

If you're a student of online marketing and you're looking to build a business, or you're looking to grow and scale an existing business, you likely know the importance of automation. On the other hand, you may be intimidated by what seems like a complex system to implement. I can promise you, if you take the time to invest in resources like this one, and in learning and improving your automation, you will see the benefits in your business.

So read this book carefully, because automation is the future of marketing. And Troy Broussard is not only a leading teacher in marketing automation, but he's also a practitioner himself operating at the cutting edge.

If marketing automation is important for your business, Troy is someone you should follow closely and this book is a great place to start.

Enjoy!

Ryan Levesque

Author, #1 National Best-Selling Book, Ask.

www.AskMethod.com

ISBN 978-1-5399108-6-2

For information on quantity discounts, speaking, interviews or training engagements, please email the publisher at troy@ismastery.com.

Requests for permissions should be addressed to the author at 13506 Summerport Village Parkway, #714, Windermere, FL 34786, or via email, troy@ismastery.com.

Printed in the United States of America

Infusionsoft Mastery

www.ismastery.com

Troy Broussard

Dedicated to:

Edward Lova Williams

Ed Williams, or "papa," as he was known to me, was my maternal grandfather. He was born September 19th, 1919, the youngest of nineteen children (yes, 9/19/1919), in the tiny little town of Pink, Oklahoma. He was one of the hardest working men I ever knew, and, though he was my grandfather, he was like a second father to me.

Long before today's technological definition of an entrepreneur was ever created, he, more than anyone else, taught me the meaning of what it was to be an entrepreneur in service of others. At different points in his career, he drove an ambulance, drove a tow truck, and flew his little Cessna 172 to drop supplies into grief stricken areas during the 1964 flood in Humboldt County, California. He was always looking to help and serve others, sometimes disguised as doing business.

He taught me the meaning of perseverance, integrity, determination and independence. But I will always remember my grandfather for his kind eyes, smile and loving heart. I miss you every day, Papa.

TABLE OF CONTENTS

ABOUT TROY

I grew up far too fast, and, in many ways, my childhood was cut short when, at 10, my 18-year-old sister, Traci Janine Broussard, was killed in a traffic accident which was the result of a bizarre set of circumstances that all culminated into the perfect storm that somber day in 1980.

Though I miss my sister dearly, I am eternally thankful to her and the profound influence she has had on my entire life. Yes, I grew up too quickly. Yes, I lost some of my childhood. Yes, it was a difficult time for our entire family. But through it all, I learned the power of NOW and living as if there were no tomorrow.

I have lived a very full and blessed life thanks, in large part, to my sister. She gave me the courage to move away from home at 13 years old and attend a private boarding school. That taste of independence, which came from a desire to attend the school she had once attended, led to an insatiable quest for self-sufficiency, travel and learning that has defined my entire life.

At 16, I traveled to Brasil (native spelling) as an exchange student, and, at 17 with a parental waiver, enlisted into the Navy's Nuclear Propulsion program onboard submarines. Then later earning an NROTC scholarship to the Illinois Institute of Technology, and a quick trip down the path of hard knocks, as I dropped out of college and began my own path.

I have been fortunate to have had many careers in my life, from being a software salesman at Egghead (oh, remember the days?), to a self-taught programmer working at Encyclopædia Britannica, a land developer, a general contractor, a cabinet shop owner, an SEO services provider, a trainer, a coach, a consultant and a SaaS company owner. I have been very blessed indeed, but I was not lucky. Those are two very different things.

I believe in opening your mind and your own doorways – creating your own luck. My former SEO company – which grew to a multi-million-dollar company in 22 months and to a staff of 110 during that same timeframe – was built while I lived overseas, with a terrible Internet connection, in a third-world country, and during the worst economic depression since *The Great Depression*. You <u>CAN</u> create your own economy!

It is amazing what the universe will conspire to bring to you when you're simply willing to first provide for others with no expectation.

I'm an instrument-rated private pilot and an avid family man who loves to travel. I make my homes on the West Coast in Southern Oregon, the East Coast in Florida and in São Paulo, Brasil – frequently traveling between them. Recently I've been working on the road while traveling full time with the family throughout the USA for a planned yearlong adventure. At 45, at the time of writing this book, I can tell you I cherish, first and foremost, freedom, and strive to continually improve and refine my three businesses to provide ever more freedom while still growing.

I'm blessed to have a beautiful, loving wife, Edina, who is the love of my life. Ever supporting and uplifting, I've rarely ever seen her upset. Not one of those false happy people, but, rather, a strong, quietly confident in her own skin, rock of eternal contentment and happiness. She wakes up happy and content each and every day, and is the absolute joy of my life. Together, we have two children, and I have two older children who live with their mom in Brasil and frequently travel to spend time with us several times a year.

Passion. Freedom. Family. That about sums me up.

ACKNOWLEDGMENTS

It is very humbling to write a book. It is such a contradictory set of emotions for me. On one level, I feel I have many books already written in my head, waiting their turn to come out and transform into physical form. At the same time, though, I absolutely know my knowledge, beliefs and experiences are not uniquely mine.

I have had tremendous, influential relationships during my 45 years, and I know they have dramatically shaped everything I have done. Many of the core concepts I teach have been derived from the works of others in small and large part. I think anyone who does not admit as much is completely out of touch with his own smallness.

On a personal note, no one has been there for me like my mom, Marjean Lovay Broussard. She has been more than a mother to me; she has been my best friend throughout my life. Having made millions and lost it all twice, my life has been a journey of ups and downs, as I am sure yours has, as well. Through it all, though, my mom has always been my most steadfast supporter.

My loving and lovely wife, Edina de Oliveira Broussard, has been my rock, my true love, *minha luz* (my light) and inspiration. My four children, Thales, Julia, Olivia and Nicolas; my compass.

I tragically lost my eighteen-year-old sister, Traci, when I was just ten years old, but she has had a profound impact on my life and my success. At the young age of ten, I learned what I consider to be life's most important lesson – tomorrow is never guaranteed.

That lesson has been the biggest gift in my life, and for that, I am eternally thankful to you, big sister. You gave me a drive and intensity unmatched by 99% of the people I've encountered in life, and taught me to live in the "now," leaving nothing undone or unsaid.

My grandparents, Edward Lova Williams and Marjorie Irene Williams – "Nana" and "Papa" - gave me the solid foundation in life to really understand the strength of family. Nana especially reinforced that strength as the matriarch of our family. Nana and Papa, your lessons and love are forever woven into the very fabric of who I am.

Benedito Maximo de Conceição entered my life at the age of sixteen, as I traversed the hemisphere to go live in Brasil (native spelling) as an exchange student. I don't even know how to describe the profound impact Maximo has had on my life. One part father, one part wise businessman, one part life-long sage, three parts eternal friend and mentor – Maximo has shaped everything I have done since. I would best describe him as my *Socrates* from the book, *Way of the Peaceful Warrior*, by Dan Millman.

Isaia Di Bello believed in me when no one else did. After just losing everything I owned in 2008 – my plane, my Harley, multiple residences, a handful of land development companies, several million dollars, and my marriage of seven years – Isaia believed in me, invested in me and encouraged me with tough love and, often firm, guidance. Within two years I, along with my then-business partner and close friend, Mike Pereira, had rebounded to build my second multi-million-dollar company - an online SEO company with a team of more than one hundred ten on staff. While Isaia was not involved in that, his belief to invest in me months earlier is what gave me the self-confidence to do it all over again.

John Sanpietro is my partner in one of my three businesses, and a dear friend. Ever since we met, we formed a bond that has remained strong to this day. I'm not sure two people can be fundamentally more different than John and I, and yet so drawn to the same path. We may have entirely different approaches, skill sets and methods, but our core passion is strongly congruent. John's perspective, wisdom and, most of all, friendship, have been a vital part of my life these past years.

I can't begin to think of John without acknowledging my friend and mentor, Ryan Lee. It was at a Ryan Lee event, where both John and I were speaking, that we met – one of those small moments in life where you take a risk, choose to do something different, and it forever changes the trajectory of your life. Ryan's impact over the years since has been strong and profound. Although Ryan and I are, in many ways, opposites in our approach – his focus on ultra-simplicity and mine on robust, often sophisticated, marketing automation – I have always listened to his "keep it simple" philosophy in everything I do. More than that, however, has been his constant reminder that integrity trumps all, and to always remember to serve first.

Tom Beal has been my most trusted advisor in recent years; a dear friend, a mentor and an amplifier to that often quiet voice of reason tap dancing in my head. In recent years, no one has had as profound of an impact on my life, my mindset and my happiness than Tom, whom I consider a life-long, true friend, as well as colleague.

Nick Kulavic has become my partner and programming cohort. Always a fresh perspective, earnest desire to serve and a keen eye for delivering value, Nick's become a dear friend.

Adam Spiel and Tony Tiefenbach have both been steadfast mentors, colleagues and friends through the years. Their candor, guidance, compassion and energy have become a driving force for me. Adam has the incredible knack for creating cutting-edge, yet simple approaches to solving complex marketing problems. Tony is the best sales mind I've ever worked with – and I've worked with many of the best in the industry. His style and approach has always resonated most with me.

Kevin Nations challenged me to consider a new paradigm to all that I do. The year I spent in his tutelage was one of the toughest of my professional life. He challenged me – oftentimes, in ways I only today have begun to understand – to step out of my own way, to be open to a simpler approach, to be willing to have a profound impact. One of the most brilliant minds of the time, Kevin taught (and continues to teach) me to be true to myself, my integrity and balance of life.

Ryan Levesque has taught me to unlearn what I thought I knew, look at the same problem from different perspectives and to constantly refine and improve. He is one of the true leaders and mentors who can teach without speaking. He creates channels, avenues, unites authorities and colleagues, teaches through his actions – so much is there to learn. Yes, he has courses and trainings, a best-selling book, and his own philosophy to marketing, but to teach silently through example is the ultimate quest of any great leader.

MaryEllen Tribby has been a personal friend, mentor and inspiration for me for the past couple of years. Her razor sharp business insights and natural talent for cutting straight to the chase, eliminating confusion and providing absolute clarity have been a tremendous dose of wisdom for me.

Ken McArthur has been a friend, a trusted advisor and kindred soul who is always there to lend a hand. There are many, many other marketers and businessmen and women who I have worked with over the years who have greatly influenced my trajectory and success. This list is in no particular order whatsoever, as each have contributed in great ways to my approach to business and marketing. Some have been friends for years. Others I may have shared just one brief encounter in my life that triggered a profound shift for me. Regardless, all are cherished.

So much gratitude goes out to you Perry Marshall, Chris Brisson, Bill Harris, Frank Kern, Kevin Rogers, Sean Wander, Keith Baxter, Ezra

Firestone, Dori Friend, John Lee Dumas, Dean Hunt, John Cornetta, Matthew Peters, Justin Krane, Toby Alexander, Brian G. Johnson, Megan Daves, David Frey, Troy Greenberg, Steven Greene, Stu McLaren, Tony Rubleski, Chris Farrell, Rob Burns, Andrrea Hess, Kristopher Marek, Rachel Wall, Marc Feinberg, Satyen Raja, Dennis Linkletter, Steve Trang, Mike Wozniak, Glenn Dietzel, Daniel Vetter, Eric Lofholm, Dustin Briley, Paul Kirchoff, Travis Jones, Darren Casey, Kathy Cregan, Greg Rollet, Joel Comm, Ryan Stewman, Nic Lucas, Jasmine Platt, Mitch Axelrod, Seth Larabee, Armand Morin, Leanne Ely, Jack Born, Steve Blom, Laura Betterly, Travis Jenkins, James Wedmore, Jason Fladlien, Eelco de Boer, Roland Frasier, Ted McGrath, Robert Michon, Gauher Chaudhry, Sami Fab, Donald Wilson, and Jit Uppal.

Thank you all for your wisdom, guidance and insights that have shaped my life.

Troy A. Broussard

CHAPTER 1

Introduction

"You can have everything in life you want if you will just help enough other people get what they want."

-Zig Ziglar

Infusionsoft is the single most powerful tool for small businesses today. I believe this so much that I personally run all three of my businesses on Infusionsoft, develop SaaS apps (jointly with co-founder Nick Kulavic), provide services for Infusionsoft, teach, train and speak on Infusionsoft and even run a high-end Efficient Profits Mastermind (jointly with my business partner John Sanpietro) which largely revolves around Infusionsoft and email marketing automation.

That being said, it is not for everyone and neither is this book. I learned a long time ago that trying to be everything to all people is a waste of time. I think you'll find me refreshingly candid and direct in this book. I don't shy away from calling out the pink elephant in the room, and I discuss topics with the good, the bad and the ugly in mind.

This book is a Best Practices and strategic guide. I make no attempt to turn this into a step-by-step "how to" book for every feature in Infusionsoft. If that's what you're looking for, there are other books out there that do a great job at that already.

Instead, this book is about going beyond the basics. We're stepping out of the "how to," and into the world of "what works best." We'll even dip our toes into "what the best marketers in the industry do."

This is in no way a criticism of the "how to" style books. I believe there is a place for both, but at some point you grow beyond that as your business expands and look for higher level strategic guidance. That is the need I seek to serve in this book.

Realistic Expectations

I said that I call out the pink elephant and don't hide from the tough topics, so let's just nail one of those on the head right now.

I've heard the term "confusionsoft" used in the industry a lot. Partially because it is, admittedly, clever. Also, as a great comedian (and even better copywriter) as well as a dear friend of mine, Kevin Rogers will tell you, "there's a lot of truth in comedy". Yes, I get that.

After working with 100's of businesses on Infusionsoft over the years, however, I can honestly tell you that those who find Infusionsoft confusing are generally confused about the systems (or lack thereof) in their business. Now, I'm not talking about the little interface quirks or design flaws, etc... but rather I'm talking about high level confusion with the way things work, with Campaign Builder, with the approach to automation as a whole.

Infusionsoft is a blank canvas, and therein lies the problem. You're free to build whatever you need. The problem is, you have to build it! I think that fact alone is what leaves many confused. They expect technology to solve their business problems, but the truth is technology is merely an accelerant.

I want you to think of your business as a fire and technology as gasoline. Infusionsoft is the gas you throw on the already burning fire that will help you explode your business growth. However, if your business is just smoldering and does not have even a flame of growth, Infusionsoft cannot help you (nor can any other technology), just like gas on smoldering debris will not create a fire.

Is Infusionsoft flawed? Absolutely. It has become a bit stagnant in development the past couple of years and others in the industry have begun to catch up with it. However, the key words are catch up. Infusionsoft has led the small business marketing automation segment of the market for years, and even today, its Campaign Builder is not just on par with the competition, but far surpasses them. While there are many things that need to be improved, Infusionsoft is the best of breed and remains my number one recommended solution.

Who is This Book For

This book is specifically written for you if you have ever felt amazed and slightly perplexed by the features and power of Infusionsoft. If you firmly believe in the power it wields, but at times feel you're just not sure of the best way to use it or need some guidance on how to get the most out of it, this book is for you.

If you believe in investing in yourself, your business and your results by continued learning with an open mind and hearing outside perspectives, then this book is for you.

Like many in the Infusionsoft world, you've probably invested lots in your business and getting your Infusionsoft systems optimized and running smoothly (or as smoothly as you know how to make them). You may have even been burned a couple of times by consultants in the industry, who perhaps steered you wrong or charged you a ton for something that produced little or no value for you. If you find yourself in that situation, then this book is definitely for you.

Most of all, if you value your time above all else, including your income, this book is definitely for you. And I congratulate you for understanding that with more time you can produce more income. Time is my number one asset in life. Everything I do and teach is about how to leverage one's time more efficiently, and that is why I believe so earnestly in Infusionsoft and the leverage it can provide.

Who This Book Is Not For

If you're a debater and not an action taker, this is probably not the book for you. Most all of the concepts put forth in this book will require you to take action if you want to see improvements and results. I find that some would rather analyze things to death and argue the merits of a point rather than simply trying it out. If that's you, this is probably not your best resource.

My goal is to inspire you to see more, to reach higher, to create more, to inspire others, to achieve more and, most importantly, create more impact on those you serve in your market - whatever it may be. I firmly believe we all have unique gifts and talents and it is our charter to bring those to the masses. It is not about extracting the most money from them we can, but rather serving them at the highest level. It is with that spirit I write this book. The spirit of serving you and your business, so that you, in turn, can serve your clients and customers.

That assumes, however, you have a business that is deserving - one that is meant to provide value, inspire and serve. If you're reading this book to learn "some hacks" to make more money from your list as opposed to learning a more effective strategy so you can serve your market better, well, you may find that my message simply doesn't resonate with you.

All throughout my career, whether it was as a programmer for Encyclopædia Britannica, an independent contractor, a cabinet shop owner, a land developer, an SEO service provider or now as a speaker, author, business owner, mentor and coach, I've always made serving others my first priority. I firmly believe and practice the Zig Ziglar quote that says, "You can have everything in life you want if you will just help enough other people get what they want."

Some Assumptions of This Book

The first assumption is that you're using Infusionsoft. As the title implies, this book is specifically tailored to the Infusionsoft platform. If you're not yet using Infusionsoft, however, that doesn't mean there's not a lot to learn here or that this book won't be relevant to you if you are in the consideration phase and evaluating it.

I'm also assuming you are using the full and complete version of Infusionsoft. Personally, I don't even recommend buying the other, "lesser" versions of Infusionsoft. I feel the lower priced or starter versions of Infusionsoft are really just somewhat crippled versions of the core product and offer no compelling price difference to justify their missing features.

That doesn't mean this book won't be valuable to you if you use one of the basic versions of Infusionsoft. Most of this book will absolutely be on target and applicable for all versions of Infusionsoft. It just means some things mentioned may not be feasible if you're using a starter version.

You'll Need More

If you truly wish to become an Infusionsoft master and radically improve the level of efficiency, automation and systemization of your business and your marketing, you will have to accept the fact that Infusionsoft can't do it all by itself. There are a variety of tools, API libraries, apps and software that integrate with Infusionsoft to extend its capabilities.

The best in this industry will use various tools and extensions for Infusionsoft. They value their time above all else, and know it is far less expensive to spend a little money on a tool that gets thing done faster, rather than saving a little money in the short-term, but wasting far more valuable time. They understand they'll lose far more money in the long-run without the tool. The most proficient Infusionsoft users I know invest heavily in enhancing the abilities of Infusionsoft and customizing them to their particular business and marketing needs.

This book is not written to be a marketing piece for my tools and services, but I won't purposely shy away from mentioning them either. I've read many books that bombard you with their stuff - to the point that it feels just like a marketing piece instead of a book with value. That's not my approach. At the same time, though, I do run an Infusionsoft specific SaaS company (jointly with my partner Nick Kulavic) that designs and creates tools specifically to eliminate some of the pains and definitely to expand the gains of Infusionsoft. So, I will, from time to time, mention them to you in the context of serving you and the needs of your business.

Lastly, if you have not yet purchased Infusionsoft and are reading this book partly in evaluation or consideration, I would highly recommend that you seek out an ICP (Infusionsoft Certified Partner) to discuss your situation. Whether it be me personally, or someone else in the Infusionsoft Certified Partner community, I highly recommend you purchase Infusionsoft from a very qualified Infusionsoft Certified Partner rather than from Infusionsoft directly.

Successful and quality Infusionsoft Certified Partners will be much more devoted to your cause and success than a Kickstart specialist at corporate. The fact is, Infusionsoft Kickstarts are quite good, but they cannot live up to the quality an experienced real-world specialist can provide.

Corporate may charge less or be a little more friendly with payment terms, but, as they like to say in Brasil, "o barato sai caro." That's Portuguese, and translates roughly to "going cheap is expensive." Infusionsoft is a complex beast, and you simply do not want to evaluate how you purchase and implement it by the "cheapest" offer you can find. If you do, you're likely to spend many times that initial investment down the road in terms of a slower learning curve, less than ideal implementation or simple opportunity cost due to lack of knowledge.

Remember that Infusionsoft is a blank canvas when you first purchase it. Getting it set up properly in the beginning will have a lot to do with getting the desired result in the end. It is much harder to go back and redo something than to simply do it right the first time around.

If you follow the guidance in this book, though, I'm confident you'll be able to get more out of Infusionsoft than you probably thought possible!

CHAPTER 2

Core Concepts for Infusionsoft Mastery

"Timely, specific and justified - the three driving forces behind
Responsive Engagement that make it so effective."

To truly master Infusionsoft, you must understand the core concepts of effective, response-based marketing and how Infusionsoft implements them. Infusionsoft is merely a technology, and that means all it can really do is *grease the gears*.

What it cannot do is single-handedly transform a failing business to a profitable one. Nor can it transform a bad business idea into a good one. What Infusionsoft does is simply accelerate the pace of whatever path you are on.

If you have a solid business that is working, Infusionsoft can make it work better and faster, just like adding grease to the gears of a mechanical system reduces friction. However, if you have a business that is failing, with poor support or inadequate profit margins, Infusionsoft will simply accelerate your demise. Sorry to say, but I'd rather you not buy Infusionsoft with false expectations.

So, to really get the most out of Infusionsoft, you need to understand its strengths and play to them. I'm a big practitioner of the Law of 80/20, or Pareto's Principle, and one of my all-time favorite and must-read book recommendations for any marketer is Perry Marshall's book, "80/20 *Sales and Marketing.*" To get the most out of Infusionsoft, you really need to understand the 20% that will get you 80% of the returns you desire in your business.

A Goal Completion System

Infusionsoft is a system designed around goals and their completion. When you design a campaign in the Campaign Builder, you really need to step back and think of the goals you're trying to achieve. I teach workshops on Campaign Builder and Infusionsoft, and I'm always amazed at what I see.

I can always break down the participants into one of two categories. Those who:

- Create a sketch of the campaign first

- Just jump in and try to design it all on the fly

The people who struggle the most are the ones who fail to take just a few minutes before jumping into the tool and sketch out what they want to accomplish. The problem with this approach is it doesn't allow you to see the big picture before you get lost in the details. Rather than just preach at you via this book, let's walk through an example together so you can understand this concept.

Stage Goals

What separates Infusionsoft from the likes of an AWeber, or Constant Contact, or any other non-marketing automation based email system, is the concept of goal achievement. Infusionsoft is designed to help you break down your overall marketing goal of selling a product into a smaller set of stage goals.

If you were embarking on a mission to lose 50 pounds, for example, you'd be wise to focus on the first 5. In other words, break up the overall goal into smaller, logical stages of progression.

Stage goals are necessary steps that must happen prior to completing the main goal. For example, if you're doing a webinar, someone can't buy your product if they don't take the small first step of registering for the webinar. That act of registering for the webinar would be considered a stage goal. Then, the subsequent and logical stages would follow: attended the webinar, saw the offer, watched the replay, purchased, etc. Each of these steps would be small stage goals progressing to the overall goal of the campaign: a purchase of your product initiated from the webinar.

Step #1 - Layout the Wireframe Map

For this scenario, let's consider a marketing campaign that is registering people for a webinar, and then selling them a $5k product. Let's see how this might look when we consider the goals involved:

- Register for the webinar

- Attend the webinar

- Watch the replay if they don't attend

- Buy our product

If we step back and look at it a bit further, we will realize this list is probably too short. There are many other smaller goals that would need to exist in this process. So, let's refine it a bit further:

- Download case study PDF to stir up excitement for the upcoming webinar

- Watch a case study video prior to attending the webinar to see some results they might obtain

- Register for the webinar

- Fill out a survey to segment registrants by interest

- Get their Phone # for text alerts, and, if they don't provide it, give them an extra bonus incentive to do so

- Attend the webinar

- Watch the replay if they don't attend

- Book a call with us to discover how our product can help them

- Buy our product

If you are visual (like me) and would like to see what this might look like, here's a link to a sample campaign structure you can examine:

http://www.ismastery.com/sample

Defining the goals is really an iterative process. You want to step back and list out these stage goals from A to Z before you jump into Infusionsoft and just start willy-nilly creating a campaign. Doing it this way will create a much more structured and well-designed campaign.

If you are more of a visual person, another approach is to simply open up Campaign Builder, create a new campaign that will never be published and use it as a blank canvas just to sketch out the flow of these goals and steps. Personally, this is the way I do it. I create one campaign that I name "XYZ – wireframe," (where XYZ is the project I'm working on), and just drag the goals and a sequence between them, laying out the progression of stage goals I'll need from left to right.

Then, I create a new campaign altogether and start the actual process of building out the marketing sequences. You can do this easily by simply saving the wireframe campaign as a copy and renaming it for your actual campaign. One is the "map," and that wireframe map is left alone and used for reference. The second campaign is where I actually do the work. You must resist the urge to edit within your original wireframe and just morph it into the final campaign. If you do, you'll lose your frame of reference. Having that wireframe to go back to, helps keep your actual campaign clean and focused.

Step #2 - Optimize Each Stage

After we have this wireframe stage goal map laid out, we then begin to break it down from left to right (or top to bottom, if you made a list). So, as an example, our first stage goal is to get them to download the free case study PDF. From a marketing perspective, this would likely translate into a few emails in a sequence over a few days. Let's imagine that it was four emails we trickle out to them over the next ten days.

Now, here again, is where Infusionsoft really differs from traditional linear email marketing systems. The beauty of being a goal completion based system, and using stage goals, is we can progress people from A to Z at their own pace - giving them what they want, when they want it, and as fast as they want it.

For example, let's consider the first stage goal of registering for the webinar.

We may create four emails that will be potentially delivered over ten days. However, because Infusionsoft is goal completion based, we will know when they register for the webinar (via the application of a tag) and complete that goal immediately. This means if they register for the webinar after the first email, there is no need to nag them with the next three emails. We can now skip over the remaining emails and straight to the next stage goal, and build their desire to attend the upcoming webinar, by providing them with some compelling case studies.

This skipping behavior is controlled at the sequence level within Campaign Builder. In the bottom left area of a sequence, there is a little colored box that is either blue or green. Infusionsoft defaults to the blue "stops immediately" behavior on sequences which is this skipping behavior I've discussed. There is also, however, an option for "runs until complete" which will finish all of the emails in the sequence even if a goal is achieved.

I can tell you that I almost never use this "runs until complete" approach and I'm very glad that the default is the "stops immediately" behavior. One good example for the "runs until complete" behavior, however, would be for a fulfillment campaign where you want to ensure that they receive all of the necessary emails even if they complete a downstream goal.

This concept of skipping over unnecessary emails (goal based achievement), though seemingly so simple, is one of the cornerstones of Infusionsoft automation that allows for a very personal approach to email delivery - getting what they want, when they want it. If they respond slowly, they'll get more emails. If they take action quickly, they'll get fewer. To fully take advantage of Infusionsoft, you need to shift your mindset when you design campaigns to really focus on achieving goals, not just delivering content. That is why I spent so much time above showing you how to break down marketing campaigns into goals. When you truly embrace this concept, Infusionsoft begins to come alive, and your email marketing turns personal.

Clarifying Stage Goals

If this entire concept of stage goals seems a bit confusing to you, let me provide you with an analogy that I use when teaching this concept in person. I want you to imagine that you want to cross a river and that it is about thirty feet wide – far too wide for you to just jump across. You don't want to get your feet wet, so you decide to grab a large rock and throw it about three or four feet in front of you so that you can step onto it. You then walk out onto it and throw out another large rock three or four feet in front of the first rock, and so on. What you get is a series of small rocks that allow you to walk across the shallow river without getting wet.

This is exactly how stage goals work. You create a series of smaller, bridging goals all aligned towards your primary goal. They are simply designed to advance you towards your destination but do so in small increments.

Getting Personal, Timely and Specific

The goal of email marketing should be - first and foremost - to establish a personal relationship with your reader. Notice the two key words in the phrase: *personal* and *relationship*. You want your email to feel as if it were written by a friend, not as though it was an antiseptic hospital communication - cold, aloof and uninteresting.

You can leverage the power of Automation to make your emails much more personal, but you do have to put a little effort into it. There are several different tools at your disposal. Become familiar with them and use them in your email marketing. In one form or another, all of these come down to personalization.

One of the easiest ways to get more personal is to become time sensitive in your emails. For example, if you're sending out your email at 8:00am, then, perhaps, start your email with, "Good morning," or, even better, in the body of the email, reference something about "this morning." This is even more subtle, and subtle is good. The point of this very slight form of personalization is to make the email feel as if it were just written. Try to make a point of weaving this form of timeliness into your emails.

Another way of making email more conversational is to reference timely events. We talked about how Infusionsoft is a goal achievement system, so use that to your advantage. The first email after a goal has been achieved is the perfect opportunity for you to do this. You know the event was just achieved, so reference it in the email, and do so in a way that feels casual and timely.

Let's say you have a four-part email series designed to get the contact to watch the first video in a video series. Structurally, this might look like this: a webform to capture the lead, followed by a sequence of four emails with timers in between, leading to a Link Click Goal, which would be followed by another sequence of emails for the second video.

The perfect opportunity to get personal and to make a timely reference to a recent event would be in the very first email after the Link Click Goal. At that particular point, we know they just clicked to watch video one. We know what they did and we know when they did it. This gives us the perfect chance to make a personal and timely reference to a recent event. This will allow our communication with them to be much more personal.

You could say something like, "So, ~Contact.FirstName~, what did you think? I really wanted to get some feedback on the video you saw yesterday so I can make sure it covered the most important questions you might have. How did I do? Anything I didn't cover you'd like to know?

If so, ~Contact.FirstName~, can you do me a quick favor and just reply and tell me your thoughts?"

In this email, we're taking advantage of the fact we know they just watched the video **yesterday** and we're having a **conversation** with them. The tone feels conversational, and it is both timely and specific because we are using words and phrases like, "yesterday" and the "video you saw." I also work their name into the email copy a couple of times, but in a subtle and casual way. Not "Dear ~Contact.FirstName~" - that's cold and corporate feeling. You want the email tone to be casual and nonchalant - it should feel like a note sent from a friend.

There are several ways you can be timely and reference recent personal events like this in your copy. Make it your priority as you write your emails. Ask yourself, "how could I make this more personal?" and, "is there anything they just did I can refer to?" Also, "is there any custom data or custom field I can merge into this email to make it feel even more specific?" Lots of times, there is.

As you build out your Infusionsoft app, using custom fields becomes almost second nature. Custom fields allow you to store any data you want on the contact record. In auditing hundreds of Infusionsoft client apps over the years, however, I can tell you the problem is most people use this personal information only trivially. It tends to be a "write once" type mentality. By that I mean most Infusionsoft users will store data into custom fields for reporting, but will very rarely, if ever, reference that data later. Worse yet, and this is the real cardinal sin, it is very rarely used for personalization of email copy. That is probably the single biggest lost opportunity.

I can't even begin the conversation of personalizing your communication without referring you to the best book on the topic. It is written by my friend and mentor, Ryan Levesque. The book is entitled, "Ask," and it is a must read for anyone in business today. It is especially critical for Infusionsoft users. Ryan is the premiere industry expert in using surveys to segment your audience, as well as identify what they most want to buy. The book goes into detail defining the methodology behind conducting effective surveys, as well as how to use that survey data to create immensely personal and highly specific email copy. Best of all, everything he teaches can easily be implemented within Infusionsoft.

Unfortunately, when most use custom data, (assuming the data is merged into emails at all), it is almost always done in a very formal and disclosed way, rather than casually inserted. For example, you'll see something like this:

"Dear ~Contact.FirstName~,

You replied in your survey that:

~Contact._SurveyResponse1~

People that answer that way generally..."

This is not a casual or conversational style of email. First off, it begins formally with a "Dear ~Contact.FirstName~," which just doesn't feel natural. Then, it really calls attention to the fact data is being merged into the email - almost as if it were a form letter. The merge fields and blocked structure are quite obvious.

The real key to success with merging personal data into an email is to do it in a completely nonchalant and casual way, imperceptible and unnoticed by the user. Again, to really drill in this point - because it is so critical - let's consider an example.

As part of the Indoctrination campaign for new users who sign up to your list, let's say you ask them to take a survey. Now, I'm not trying to make this a case on how to create a perfect survey, so please excuse the crudeness of the survey, but my goal is to illustrate how to pivot the data into a very personal nature.

Let's say one of the questions in the survey asks them to list their income goals for their business. The categories are: < 100k, 100K to $250k and $250K or more. The mistake I see all of the time, and I do mean ALL of the time, is people will store the data in the custom fields the exact same way they asked the question. So, in the custom field, it would have "< 100k" as an example.

How can you then use that data in a meaningful and casual way in a conversational tone within your email? You can't. Instead, what if you translated the value into a meaningful phrase you could casually work into the body of your email. Something like, "six-figure business."

For example, "You know, one of the common mistakes I see with business owners that are working hard to create a **six-figure business** is that they..." - you get the idea.

The point is, by using custom data acquired through surveys, questions and other means, and storing it in a way that allows you to personalize your emails, you'll really resonate with their pain points and unique situation, but you'll do it in a very casual way. The contact will come away thinking, "wow, this guy (or gal) really gets me!" rather than feeling like they're reading generic copy written for anyone. The key to all of this, though, is to make it feel casual and incorporate it into your copy naturally. By the way, I bolded the phrase in that example only to highlight it to you. You clearly would NOT want to do that in your copy. The point is to make it blend in and not call specific attention to it.

Take that example further, and combine multiple fields of information into a couple of sentences. Perhaps you reference their job type, or one of their major life goals. Now you have an extremely personal email that would feel like it came from a good friend who "just got them." Imagine if the copy were something like this:

"Hey Paul, good to see you on the webinar **yesterday**. I **saw your question** about XYZ product and I know you're concerned if it will work for you in **direct sales**. One of the biggest needs when you're struggling to hit that **six-figure level** in your business is **becoming more efficient**."

Take a look at the bold and underlined text. In this example, I've made several merges based upon questions asked, timely references and knowledge of a specific event. I reference the webinar he attended yesterday. I also take note that he asked a question. This is something we can do with automation and elegant API integrations. For example, our MyFusionHelper.com app (available with a free trial at http://ismastery.com/free) integrates with GotoWebinar. It allows you to store the questions someone asked into a custom field, or even create a dynamic segment and tag people who asked a question. In fact, the software even allows you to segment people based upon the length of the questions they ask or whether or not they attended the webinar.

Next, I reference his type of business - direct sales. This could have been a response from a survey about his business and goals. Again, as shown in the prior example, I reference his income level and desire to grow his business to the six-figure level.

Finally, I reference his selected pain point or desire to become more efficient (again a reference to a question answered during a survey).

In this example, I've used several different dynamically merged fields that would have several different values applied to many people with different goals, business sizes and responses. With creative use of custom fields, and decision diamond branching in Campaign Builder, you can create very robust and super dynamic content like this to really speak to your contacts. Creating highly specific content like this - if done properly - can triple your marketing results in a given campaign as compared to generic copy.

Ryan Levesque's book, "*Ask*," goes into much more on this topic, and my brief discussion in this chapter is but a drop in the bucket compared to his very elegant and detailed approach to segmentation through surveys and personalized communication. He's taught me much in this arena. I've always used a degree of personalization and segmentation in all of my marketing, but going to the level he does really magnifies your results dramatically.

So, remember these three principals: personal, timely and specific. To really drill this into your mindset towards automation enhanced copywriting, I want you to simply go through some of the copy in the most important campaign sequence of your business. Rate each email on a simple three-point scale (1=poor, 2=ok, 3=good) for its usage of personalization, timeliness and specificity.

I like using a numeric scale to rate things like this because it adds a degree of objectivity to it. It also allows you to numerically track your progress over time. I recommend you make this a regular practice when critiquing your copy, as well as your split tests - which transitions us nicely to our next core concept.

Split Testing

Split testing is the practice of evaluating the effectiveness of something (email copy, an offer, a price point, etc.) by dividing the traffic up equally, sending it down two different paths, and evaluating the end result. While split testing is not inherently built into Infusionsoft from a technology standpoint, or emphasized in Infusionsoft training, I do believe it is a core concept critical to marketing automation.

Automation is all about systems and efficiency. There is nothing more efficient than split testing, because, at its core, the purpose of split testing is really to get more from what you already have.

If you have an email series going out to promote a product, don't you want it to be as effective as possible? Well, with split testing, you can learn which types of subjects and which email styles and tonality work best for your list. You can create two different variations, run the test, and observe which has the bigger impact.

There are lots of methodologies to split testing, and I could write an entire book on the topic, but that's not why I'm bringing it up. The reason I'm mentioning it to you, is I believe it is a core concept you should embrace in your business and marketing automation.

The one thing, from a mindset perspective, I love about split testing is it encourages you to think of each campaign or sequence as an experiment. That is exactly how I treat every marketing campaign I create - as an experiment. I'm always testing something in every campaign. I never think of a campaign as finished. I just think of it as a work in progress. I purposely construct tests and experiments into my campaigns so I can refine and enhance them later. Even if it is a one-off campaign, by putting experimental tests into it, you can learn about your list, and use that knowledge to improve the results of your next campaign.

There are a few leading approaches to split testing I want to mention. One is the simple A/B Split Test. This is the most common form of split testing, as it simply divides the traffic up into two random segments of equal size - an "A" segment, and a "B" segment - and then tracks the results for each segment. When you have small lists, or are testing with small segments of a list, this can make the most sense.

There is another approach, called, "multivariate split testing." This is a rather advanced form of split testing which allows you to simultaneously test multiple variations (rather than just two). Multivariate split testing can be quite complex, and can require a lot of traffic in order to yield results. For those reasons, I'm not going to focus on it in this book.

Another popular split testing approach you may want to consider is a 10/10/80 Split Test. The 10/10/80 approach works great if you have a larger list and want to maximize your results. In this type of split test, it is a two-step process. The first step is to just grab 20% of your total list, and randomly split it into two segments - just like an A/B Split Test. Then, you grab the other 80% of your list, and send it to the winner from the 10/10 split.

The beauty of this type of split test is you get more positive ROI from the results. This is because you're immediately putting the split test to work for you. After you get the results from the 10/10 split, you can immediately reap the rewards from the winner with the remaining 80% of your list. This can be far more productive than sending 50% of your list to the loser - which will always be the case in a simple A/B Split Test.

The downside is if you don't have enough data going to the 10/10 split, your results may not be statistically relevant. In other words, this works best for larger lists.

How large is large enough? How small is too small? These are the subtleties split testing aficionados will debate until the wee hours of the night. There is much debate over what is and what isn't statistically relevant, and I really do not want to go down that rabbit hole in this book. The point here is to provide you with strategic guidance on the topic, and encourage you to look into it for your own best practices. Part of understanding Best Practices is to understand they have to be customized and tailored to your own usage. Split testing is definitely an example of that.

Responsive Engagement

Responsive Engagement is a phrase I've coined to describe another core concept I use and teach with Infusionsoft. It is all about escaping the linear, force-fed approach of email marketing that has dominated the industry for the past fifteen years. Responsive Engagement is about leveraging the automation capabilities of Infusionsoft to create scenarios that respond to the contacts' engagement within the system, and bubble up events or opportunities to re-engage them.

It is much easier to simply give you an example than to try and explain it conceptually. RFM (Recency - Frequency - Monetary) is an example of Responsive Engagement. RFM is a way of tracking and reporting on how recently (R) a customer has bought, how frequently (F) they buy and how much they spend (M). Typically, however, these are looked at as a reporting mechanism.

What I like to do - and why I coined this phrase of Responsive Engagement - is use that type of data as a method for responding to a contact and engaging with them, instead of just looking at it as reporting data. Let's take one of the variables of RFM as an example, and consider Recency.

Recency is designed to report on how long it has been since the customer last made a purchase. You can measure the days and report on it, so that you can improve your numbers. If your average customer recency value is 38 days, what type of marketing could you do? How could you modify your campaigns to try and reduce that average from 38 days to 23 days? That is the concept behind recency.

What I like to do, however, is create thresholds of engagement based upon recency. My concept of Responsive Engagement would lead to the creation of an automation campaign that would track the number of days since a contacts' last purchase. I would then create several thresholds at, for example, 30 days, 60 days and 90 days. At each of these thresholds, an event would fire (a goal was achieved). So, when it has hit the 30-day threshold since a purchase was made, a campaign could, for example, be automatically kicked off that sends them a 10% off coupon code valid for the next 48 hours only.

The point is to pivot the reporting data, and, instead, make it a mechanism for bubbling up events that are responsive to that contacts' actions or inactions. Now, instead of a plain top-down linear approach to our marketing, we have a more dynamic and responsive approach, that is custom tailored to how the contact has engaged with us.

A very common example of Responsive Engagement would be the traditional abandoned cart sequence. When someone starts a checkout process, and adds an item to their shopping cart, but does not complete their purchase, smart marketers will send them out an email a little while later trying to get them to come back and complete their purchase. This action is a perfect example of Responsive Engagement. You're engaging the client in response to an action they took.

If you'd like a more in-depth look at how to use RFM in your business, go here:

http://www.ismastery.com/rfm

The Recency example I listed is just one small example. There are hundreds of ways you can incorporate this concept into your marketing. Like all of the other Core Concepts, it is just as much a mindset as it is a technical approach. I encourage you to examine your marketing and business, and look for ways you could make them more responsive to your users' actions, as opposed to forced according to your will. This is what really empowers Infusionsoft - when you leverage technology with copywriting, and transform to a more situationally-aware marketing platform. You have the power to do this within Infusionsoft, but just like a finely tuned piano, it still has to be used properly in order to achieve the desired outcome.

Why is Responsive Engagement so powerful? It all comes back to engaging the contact at the right time with the right message. Because you're using an event to trigger the communication, and because that event is in response to some action they did or did not take, the communication is both timely and specific. It also has a reason for being sent. Many times, just having a reason for emailing them is enough to break down the barriers of jaded interpretation, and get them to actually read what you're sending.

Think through the example of the abandoned cart sequence. It is effective because of its timeliness - you just were at their store contemplating a purchase, and their site very fresh in your mind. It is also very effective because of its specificity. An abandoned cart email, if done effectively, will refer to the product they were just considering. This specificity can be used very cleverly in the email body and subject line to skyrocket the open and click rates.

Lastly, there is a reason or justification for the vendor to be emailing you. It is not an unsolicited email out of the blue. Rather, it is merely a continuation of a process they already initiated. So, to your contact, it makes sense. Timely, specific and justified - the three driving forces behind Responsive Engagement that make it so effective.

Get It Done Then Make It Better

This is another core concept that, unfortunately, many marketers and small business owners fail to grasp. I call it the "gotta be perfect" syndrome. Many people will struggle for days, weeks or, even, months trying to get everything just perfect before turning it on. They will fret over it, change up the logic three times over, question and second guess their approach and, ultimately, just procrastinate out of fear of what might happen.

With Infusionsoft, or any other technology system, in order to benefit from it, you have to use it. In other words, you need to put things out there and test them.

A flawed but published campaign will outperform a perfect but unpublished time every time!

I can assure you your first few campaigns will be far from perfect. I can also assure you, though, not turning them on will achieve far less! So don't be fearful about not having the perfect campaign. Instead, embrace my methodology that every campaign is an experiment. There's something to be learned.

So go out and learn! To learn, however, you have to hit, "Publish!" You have to get those campaigns out there, see some results, determine how to improve on those results and continue to move forward.

The easiest way to do this is to start simple. In the beginning, don't try to accomplish everything with your campaigns. Make them short and straightforward. As you get more accustomed to how Infusionsoft and Campaign Builder work, you'll be able to add sophistication and elegance to them. In the beginning, though, it is about volume and repetition.

I want to let you in on a little secret. Many of your campaigns simply won't work out as planned. Big shock, right? This is why it is critical you develop the mindset of, "get it done," instead of struggling with the fallacy of trying to, "get it perfect." If many of your campaigns won't work out the way you want anyway, do you really want to invest hundreds of hours into trying to get them perfect?

In the Efficient Profits Mastermind that I run jointly with my business partner, John Sanpietro, one of the methodologies we teach is F3. F3 (or

"FFF") stands for, "Fail Forward Fast." It is a mindset that accepts the premise that much of what you do will not be a huge success. So, rather than trying to make things perfect, you focus on getting them done at an MVP (minimal viable product) level of functionality as quickly as possible.

The MVP concept is one you should really spend some time researching and embracing if you're not familiar with it. MVP comes from the programming world - don't worry, I'm not going to go off on geek speak here. Programming is a very precise and painstakingly methodical process.

Traditional programmers were trained to take their time. They're "programmed" to spend a ton of effort on getting product specification documents perfect before starting the programming efforts. All of that translated into projects that never seemed to get done, and when they finally did, they were way over budget and way late. This traditional, old-school methodology for programming has given way to a more contemporary MVP approach, which is all about getting a very thin implementation functional as quickly as possible, and then, improving and enhancing it on the fly.

Build your marketing campaigns with this same MVP approach. Focus on getting them complete and testing their impact before you try to make them perfect. Doing so you will likely produce 2x or 3x more growth in your business during the same timeframe.

Continual Refinement

Continual refinement goes hand in hand with the MVP model introduced above. This is not contradictory, it is complimentary. You need to get things done quickly. At the same time, though, you need to develop a mindset that nothing is truly ever done.

I'm not trying to go all Zen on you here, and this is not purposed ambiguity. It is simply the most effective method for rapid development.

Remember, my mantra is to treat every campaign as if it is an experiment. Well, if the experiment passes the MVP model, and is successful, we want to continue to enhance it.

Let's consider that you're going to test out a new marketing campaign using the webinar model. You create your webinar, and you create a marketing campaign to support it. Until you know if your webinar itself resonates with your audience (makes some sales), it is really not worth spending too much time trying to create the perfect marketing campaign for it.

However, after you release the MVP campaign for the webinar, and you see it did, indeed, do fairly well, and make some sales, now it is time to step back and refine. This is when you really embrace the stage goal mentality I taught earlier in this chapter. Look at each stage individually, as if it were its own mini-campaign. In other words, you focus on refinement and improvement.

You start asking more questions of how you could improve the campaign. You introduce more experiments into the campaign. For example, "would text message reminders boost attendance?"

So, get it done first. Get some results. Then, go back, refine and improve. By using our F3 approach, if your webinar is a flop, at least it flopped quickly, and you didn't waste too much time. You're now free to move on to the next marketing experiment!

Wrapping It Up

This chapter has really laid out the core concepts and the mindset necessary to truly excel with Infusionsoft, and marketing automation in general. While this entire book is written with Infusionsoft in mind, these concepts are truly universal to marketing automation as a whole.

CHAPTER 3

The Five Stages of Infusionsoft Mastery

"think of each campaign or sequence you design as an experiment"

Mastery of any subject requires continued study, practice and improvement – Mastery of Infusionsoft is no different. Mastery is also not something that you ever attain, but rather continually pursue. Though I have been using Infusionsoft for years, Mastery requires chasing an ever-moving target.

Infusionsoft is continually enhanced and improved, so I must continually learn, test, adapt, and refine my techniques. Thankfully that's my problem and not necessarily yours! In other words, you don't have to master every last iota of Infusionsoft in order to get tremendous results from it in your business; and, more importantly, to create the lifestyle you desire.

At What Stage of Infusionsoft Development Are You?

As you progress towards Infusionsoft mastery, you'll go through various stages of development and growth. The same is true in any endeavor you pursue. If you want to be a pro Baseball player, there are various stages of minor leagues from Rookie and Class A leagues to Triple A. There are a lot of steps you will likely have to go through before reaching the big leagues.

The clients that I have worked with over the years that have gotten the most out of Infusionsoft have adapted a very similar systematic approach to refining their business automation systems. I've put my own spin on this to create what I call **The Five Stages of Infusionsoft Mastery**.

First off, know that not everyone will choose to go through all five stages – that's okay. Remember my motto, that there is no *one-size fits all* approach to business. So use Infusionsoft in the way that makes the most sense for you and your business.

However, Infusionsoft is a significant investment and its capabilities are incredible if you're willing to continue to go down the rabbit hole that is automation and systemization. The purpose of clearly defining these stages is to illustrate to you not only where you likely are right now, but also to show you how much further you could go, if you choose to.

Here's a quick assessment you can use to ascertain where you are now, as well as plan where you are going.

These are the Five Stages of Infusionsoft Mastery:

Stage I: Migration

You just ported your emails over from AWeber (or other legacy system), and setup your basic system level automations (expiring credit card procedures, billing automation, etc.) or, perhaps, have not yet, but plan to. You probably feel completely overwhelmed at this point and are just trying to keep your head above water with all of the moving parts.

The entire concept of Marketing Automation, while alluring, may feel a bit out of your grasp right now and you likely have chosen just to keep it simple (for now). You probably have decided that the first step is just getting off your old system, and so you're not too worried about doing things right or even better so much as you are just *"getting them done"* and off your old platform.

This is very common and, honestly, there's no real flaw in the logic. Transitioning from one system to another can be painful and slow, and the best way to do it truly is to just rip off the Band-Aid and get it done. It is not the mindset that is flawed here, but rather the one key missing ingredient that I see so often neglected.

That missing ingredient is the acknowledgement that the compromises you're making now to get it done, must be addressed with continual improvement and refinement. At this stage you likely have very little tracking, but should, at least, implement Lead Sources and Form/Campaign Tagging.

I can honestly say that after working with hundreds of clients over the past several years probably 60% of them never get beyond this first "migration" stage of their Infusionsoft evolution. This is a real shame because it expresses the very real problem that most Infusionsoft users face; they simply aren't using the power of Infusionsoft to anywhere near its potential.

Just like I personally use probably less than 20% of the features of Microsoft Word which I'm using to write this book, most Infusionsoft users also use far less than 20% of the features they have available to them. The intent of breaking this down into stages is to show you that you can and should continually look to increase your usage of Infusionsoft because every dollar you invest into efficiency and automation will probably payoff tenfold in the years to come.

Stage II: Simplistic Automation

You've gone for the 20% approach, finding low-hanging automation fruit in your campaigns, and adding some simple stage tracking. Your goal has really been to just get things moving towards a more automated marketing platform, but you realize you're really only just getting started. You're starting to see how the Core Concepts of Infusionsoft automation can help, and are just starting to implement them more.

You've likely ventured into some of the basic automations built into Infusionsoft like Billing Automation and perhaps email status automation.

It is my experience that this accounts for another 20% of the clients that I have worked with over the years. That means that 80% of those clients and Infusionsoft users have likely never progressed into Stage III or above.

This is what I like to call the "just getting started" phase of your Infusionsoft evolution. In Stage II you begin to make inroads into creating systems and begin to see the light at the end of the tunnel. So why is it that so many never progress further? Why is it that for so many that light turns into an oncoming train that derails their further progress?

I've spent a lot of time studying this phenomenon – the resistance in moving beyond this phase of Infusionsoft maturity. What I've found is that it is not for a lack of desire, nor from a lack of intent, nor even from a lack of acceptance that they need to go further with Infusionsoft. What I've found to be the two biggest reasons for paralysis at this stage come down to overwhelm and/or lack of resources (or the wrong resources).

The feeling of overwhelm is very common when embarking on a migration of this level of sophistication. There's a lot to learn in Infusionsoft and you may get to this point where you simply get comfortable with what you have. You've been able to get through the initial data conversion and so the urgency is gone, but now, as you look at the next level of tasks it just seems like there's so much to do that it becomes overwhelming.

The real trick to success is to not try and to too much at once. Remember the parable about how to eat an elephant – you do it one bite at a time. Take the same approach with Infusionsoft and you won't get overwhelmed. Instead just focus on continual improvement. Set aside a couple of hours every week to continue to improve what you've started, rather than turning it into a huge project like what you just went through with the migration, and you'll have continued success.

The second biggest reason for staying stuck at this stage is generally some sort of a resource issue. You may have started off this project fully intending to do it yourself, but have since come to the realization now that it is just more than you have the bandwidth to do. Or, perhaps, you hired a resource to assist but, as it turns out, they're just the wrong resource for the job.

Don't let this derail your efforts and progress with Infusionsoft. If this is the situation you find yourself in, then you really have two choices. Either break up the project in smaller bite size chunks and just allocate less time towards it but continue the progress, or look to add someone to your team that can do it for you.

Both of those decisions require a bit of humility and are a bit tough to swallow, and that is why many get stuck at this phase. It can be hard to admit to ourselves that we need help. Infusionsoft, however, is a significant investment and one that can repay you many times over if you implement it to its fullest. Remind yourself of that, and simply map out a path of how to proceed, even if at a slower pace than you had originally intended.

Stage III: Robust Automation

In this phase, you've taken a second pass at your campaigns, and added more sophisticated automation to them, such as abandoned cart hooks or full 3-step tracking including Referral Link Tracking. You're now actively adopting the Core Concepts of Infusionsoft automation, and it is starting to become more natural for you.

This is where most people start to get in the groove with Infusionsoft and most that make it this far, will continue to the next stage of mastery as well. You're likely to start looking for new and creative ways to implement automation campaigns in your business now and that is when Infusionsoft can really help you flourish.

Start to expand your horizons of what you can do and explore new ways to automate your business, thinking outside of the box. Look at your systems internally and look to automate them. One of the big opportunities here is looking at your daily tasks and how you can begin to leverage Infusionsoft to outsource those tasks and to automatically monitor their progress for you.

Task level automation can be one of the most powerful ways to scale your business. This is where you have to really look inward at your business practices and systems and ask yourself how you could leverage Infusionsoft to automate them.

Most people tend to think of projects rather than tasks. But if you can train yourself to break up a project into all of its component tasks instead, you'll be able to quickly see that probably 80% of those individual tasks could easily be outsourced and automated. This is how you scale your business, by taking 80% of what you do that is simple stuff and just get it off of your plate so you can focus on the more important aspects of your business.

Stage IV: Refined Automation

You've now taken a 3rd pass (or more) at your campaigns, and gone deep with split testing of email subjects and offer pricing. You're going in deep to the Referral Link Tracking now, and the Core Concepts of Infusionsoft automation marketing have become second nature. You actively implement them at every step of the process.

At this phase of your Infusionsoft maturity, you've become very good at breaking down projects into tasks and are using robust task automation in your business. You've likely begun to see many areas that Infusionsoft could be improved and have begun supplementing your business with outside tools, such as our MyFusion Helper app, to fill in the gaps in functionality.

There are really two common activities that identify that you've hit this stage. One is the that you're actively looking for other tools and apps to extend Infusionsoft. This is common when you've hit this level of sophistication in your automation marketing. Don't fret, you have not outgrown Infusionsoft, you're merely beginning to use it to its real potential and that is where the magic begins to happen.

The other common thing that begins to happen is that you begin to really see how certain features of Infusionsoft were designed with one intention but you've begun to see how they could be used creatively for an entirely different purpose. This level of understanding of Infusionsoft means that you're not just thinking of using it in the way it was intended, but you've become so familiar with its toolset that you're beginning to see how to leverage it beyond its intended purpose. This is very powerful.

An example of this would be fulfillment reports in the Campaign Builder. They're intended, very specifically, to send out a list of orders to be fulfilled by an outside company. However, once you really understand how this simple snippet works, you can see that it is really just a "queuing mechanism" and discover some other very creative uses for it.

Embrace this inquisitive mindset, thinking outside the boundaries of the original intentions of Infusionsoft. This is a very powerful level of understanding that will lead you to create much more robust automations in your business.

I like to think of Steve Jobs and his creation of such a powerful iOS system for app developers. I know that there is no way that he could have imagined all of the sophisticated apps that would be created when he designed the OS.

There is an app that allows you to stand your iPhone on its end on a level table and it controls the vibration of the phone so that it causes the phone to rotate in a smooth fashion in a complete 360 degree circle, literally "spinning" around in a circle on its end. Why? Well, it is popular with realtors to film the inside of their homes for sale with a 360 degree view. Simply put it on a table in the center of the room and you're set.

This app takes the vibrate feature of the phone, something that had a very specific and intended purpose, and uses it in a completely different and creative way to create a powerful and robust solution. That is the kind of out of the box thinking that you can use in your implementation of Infusionsoft as well.

Stage V: Sophisticated API Automation (Mastery)

You have become very efficient in your campaign automation, and your campaigns are elegant and refined. You are now looking deep into how you can continue your quest for more automation and efficiency, and have identified various areas in your internal systems that you are actively enhancing further with API level integrations and automations.

By now you are likely usindg several different apps jointly with Infusionsoft to enhance it further and may even be considering creating some custom API integrations yourself. You have likely got a wish list of features and enhancements that you have already identified as potential enhancements to your workflows and systems and are actively looking to implement them.

I've seen many people get stuck at this point as well. The reason comes down to hiring and managing developers. You may know what you want an API integration to do, but you cannot expect a developer to read your mind.

As someone who has been on both sides of the fence – both as a business owner and as a developer – I can tell you that the single biggest reason for development projects failing is in the lack of specificity of the requirements. As a business owner, you need to really spend time to be highly specific as to what you want the app to do.

If you learn to create great requirements documentation for your projects, you'll find that getting a developer to implement it properly can be quite easy. Don't just provide a couple paragraphs of information and expect that someone will be able to get inside of your mind and know every last detail of what you want. That is, unfortunately, what most people do in this situation and then are amazed that they get a poor result.

Instead, lay out the different use cases for the app or integration you need. Describe each, in detail, accounting for the different potential variables, data and potential uses. Now go beyond that and try to think of potential issues or failures that could occur and how you'd like the program to handle them. If there will be any interface in the app, make sure to sketch it out in wireframe format so that it is clear to the developer what you expect it to look like and how it should function.

The Infusionsoft API is very robust and elegant. There is almost nothing you can't do with it and the level of robust and sophisticated integrations that you can create with it can really take the automation of your internal systems to a whole new level. That can allow you to free up time and create a much more efficient business.

API development is not, however, cheap. You must really scope out a project and define it properly, including the ROI it can provide. You should be able to quantify that ROI in terms of hours of manual labor saved.

Recently, for example, for a client I was able to create a custom report in Google Sheets using our real time Google Sheets integration with MyFusion Helper, that allowed the finance department to save an average of 1.75 hours per day. At an average of $28 an hour for this particular employee resource, that means that the program would save the company, on average, $49 a work day or approximately $1,078 a month in salary. The cost of developing the custom report was $625.

So you can see it had a very definitive ROI in just the first month alone. My rule of thumb for whether a project is worth pursuing or not is whether or not you can show ROI for it within 6 to 8 months. If you can, and if the system is a standing system that will be around for years to come, then it is very much worth pursuing.

Wrapping It Up

Before going on to the rest of the book, take a few minutes to go back through The Five Stages of Infusionsoft Mastery, and rate yourself on a scale of 1 to 3, 3 being the best. Write down your score and write down the date, as well. Then re-evaluate your progress every 90 days. You can use that as a long-term goal of how to continually improve your level of mastery over Infusionsoft. This will only serve to improve your efficiency and profitability of your business, as well.

CHAPTER 4

Setup & User Management

"Tags should be thought of as sacred elements used to define, document and enforce business logic."

To save yourself a lot of grief, wasted time and effort redoing work down the road, it is important to setup Infusionsoft the right way from the beginning. I know that many reading this book will have already setup Infusionsoft, and will have to revisit the way it was done, no matter what. If that is the situation you find yourself in, then just do the best you can. Even so, taking the time now and correcting any oversights will still save you time and effort in the future.

Configuring Your Branding Center

Take the time to set up your Branding Center in Infusionsoft and stop wasting time reinventing the wheel on a daily basis. This Best Practice recommendation is so easy to do, but I find only about 15% of the client Infusionsoft apps I have audited or worked on have taken the time to do it. And the truth is, it really doesn't take all that much time to do.

The Branding Center is where you set up all of the templates for the various areas of Infusionsoft. There are templates for campaign emails, broadcast emails, single emails, follow-up sequence emails, template library emails and, even, for confirmation emails.

There are also default templates for campaign forms, legacy web forms, internal web forms, landing pages and thank you pages. You even have the ability to set up your default logo and how the Infusionsoft footer is configured in your outgoing emails.

With some of the most recent changes to Infusionsoft, introducing the mobile responsive email builder, some of these templates are no longer in the the Branding Center. You can still setup templates for the mobile responsive builder and save them, but they will appear within the email builder itself, not be in the Branding Center.

All of this seems trivial, and it is, but it still needs to get done and, sadly, most Infusionsoft users simply skip it. The problem is, by skipping over it, you're just causing yourself so much added work and grief every time you use any of these templates.

Because you haven't spent the time setting up your defaults properly, each time you use them, you'll have to change something or tweak something. Maybe it is the signature that's not set up the way you want it. Maybe it is the from email settings - that could really cause you grief if you send it out improperly. The fact is, I can realistically say only about 15% of the clients I've worked with have done this properly. That means that 85% of them are wasting a few hours each and every week redoing busy work that could have been done once and never again.

Please choose to be one of the 15% - enough said.

There Can Be Only One

I couldn't resist the title, quoting from one of my all-time favorite TV series and movies, Highlander. But the truth is, it is a pretty appropriate title when referring to the Admin User role in Infusionsoft. I know that practicality will get in the way and that you will likely need at least one other Admin as a "backup," and that's okay, as long as that other person is not actively changing configurations and/or business rules and logic that you're establishing.

This next statement, however, will probably make you fall off your rocker when you first think about it, because it is so restrictive, but it truly is a Best Practice and my highest recommendation. To avoid creating a tagging mess in your app, you simply should not allow users to set tags. There, I said it.

Tags are used in Infusionsoft for many different purposes. There are functional tags, segmenting tags, audit trail tags, campaign specific tags, engagement tracking tags, stage goal tags and tracking tags. Each of them has its own purpose. Tags are both a blessing and a curse. The blessing is that they are completely customizable. The curse is that excessive tagging is the number one reason for Infusionsoft apps performing slowly and can lead to a complete spider web mess of intertwined tagging that no one - not even the creator - can understand. Ask me how I know.

The number one thing that wastes the most time when trying to take over the cleanup or organizational restructuring of a client's Infusionsoft app is trying to figure out just what the heck is going on with the tags. Everyone - me included - creates tags on the fly as needed with the thought in mind (and the best intentions) that they will organize them and document them later. But later turns into, "when I get around to it."

I'll never forget as a child visiting my great uncle in Southern Oregon. He was a little bit of an "odd duck" and he collected all kinds of stuff, trinkets mostly, and items that didn't have much value to anyone in the world but him. To me, it was just a lot of junk, but to each his own.

Once, I looked up and saw an item on his shelf that completely perplexed me. I just had no idea what the heck it was. It was a paper plate, the kind you use for picnics, and it had the writings, "tuit" written in big block letters in the center. That's all it was. Curious, I asked my uncle what this weird "tuit" plate was.

He responded, "That's my, when I get **a round 'tuit**," he jokingly responded. Corny, yes. Cheesy, yes. But the fact is most never get "tuit." So, creating a mess with the intent of cleaning it up later is the slippery slope that leads to tagging chaos in your app and perhaps shelf loads full of junk on the wall as well!

The way to fix this is to nip it in the bud and prevent the clutter in the first place. Tags should be thought of as sacred elements used to define, document and enforce business logic. Sacred elements that must be conserved and treated with care. Sacred elements that are not to be trusted in the hands of mere mortals to play with (okay, sorry, drifted back into Highlander again). But all kidding aside, there is a lot of truth in this statement.

Tagging should be established by the system admin in accordance with the needed business logic. There should be actual thought that goes into their usage, not just flippant and casual usage.

The way to keep your system very clean and highly effective is simply to not allow people to apply tags. You can do this easily via User permissions. I can promise you that it will take some getting used to, but the process that it will force is a very good one.

Not allowing people to apply tags will force you to develop very good guidance for when and how tags are applied. That consistency will allow you to maintain a very clean and well-structured app that is easy to understand and navigate, as well as easy to generate accurate reporting.

But if people can't use tags, how can they possibly use Infusionsoft? That is always the pushback I get. Many believe this is a very idealistic approach and completely impossible. I can assure it is not and it is actually quite easy once you allow yourself to adopt the discipline of setting up systems. Also, as I said before, following this Best Practice guideline will actually make you a much better Infusionsoft user because it will force you to be very diligent in your business logic creation and enforcement. That will lead to a very systemized approach and mindset that will serve you very well with everything else (especially campaign building) that you do in Infusionsoft.

Better Alternatives to Tags

I call these alternatives, but in reality, they are the tools that were meant to be used for this purpose. The problem is that tags are so easy to use, they have become overly prolific. It is human nature to take the path of least resistance, like water flowing downhill. When we find something that works, we often don't go further - we just stick with what works. Tags do work, there are just other options that work better in certain situations.

Note Goals are one of the alternatives to tags. I see very few people using Note Goals, but that is a big mistake. Notes can not only be used within a sequence to document actions, but they can also be used as a start goal to begin a campaign. It is in this context that I'm suggesting using notes, as Note Goals.

What's very cool about Note Goals is that, once the campaign is published, they will show up as Note Templates that users can apply directly to contacts in the Interactive view.

QUICK NOTE: There are two views used to work with lists of contacts. The Interactive view is what we normally use and has all of the icons that appear dynamically as we hover over a contact in the list. The Grid view is not as commonly used, but also can be very powerful as a more standard row and column tabular structure. One of the primary benefits of the Grid view is that you can easily sort columns by simply clicking on their headings.

Creating note goals can help you launch any automation necessary inside of Campaign Builder, while simultaneously creating a very simple method for users to kick off that automation from the Interactive view or from within the contact details, as well. If they are editing a contact directly, they can also apply a note template from the contact details screen. Either way, launching a contact into an automation campaign via Note Goals is very simple and effective.

One other side benefit of using Note Goals is the fact that they are self-documenting. Not only does the Note Goal trigger off the automation, but it also saves a note onto the contact record, creating an audit trail of what happened. Yes, I know, tags also accomplish this, but it is much cleaner with notes. You can pull up the notes for a contact and see a detailed and linear timeline of what has happened to that contact. With tags, this is much more cumbersome and cryptic.

You can also create different types of notes. Very few people do this, but, by setting up your own custom note types, you can search notes for specific text and even filter them by note type as well. This allows you to not only document the contacts interactions with the system, but also to easily search for and filter those notations later.

To illustrate using Note Goals, let's talk about a practical example from one of my clients. They use Note Goals very effectively in their business to allow an administrative assistant to perform various tasks quickly and easily without having to understand when to apply and remove tags.

They have Note Goals to grant access to different products in their CustomerHub membership system, remove access, send an email to the user with their password and access details, and even use them to trigger complex API automations which can automatically process a refund or subscription cancelation. All of this is done from simple Note Goals without ever having access to individual tags. Best of all, they do not have to be trained on the business logic, all they need to do is apply a note.

Internal Forms are the second alternative to using tags. Internal Forms are used to submit forms on behalf of users in the system. They are extremely useful for repeated tasks and for creating structure to how a task is carried out.

Internal Forms, like Note Goals, can also be used to initiate automation campaigns as a start goal. It is a shame they are so rarely used, but Internal Forms are just as effective as any other goal type in Campaign Builder to start a campaign. The goal type is listed as **Submits an Internal Form** in the Goal Settings dialog box within Campaign Builder.

Internal Forms are one of the most effective ways of creating very robust and structured data entry mechanisms for your users. For people that tell me that Infusionsoft is confusing, I always ask them about how it is setup, how they use it and how many Internal Forms they are using. Almost inevitably, they answer they don't even know what an Internal Form is, much less use them.

You have the full form builder at your disposal when you use Internal Forms. That means you can create very robust data entry forms that have dropdown boxes to select desired answers, and use radio buttons that can have sophisticated branching logic attached behind them in the Campaign Builder or set tags based upon their selection.

For example, one of the things I will typically do for many clients is create a *New Contact* internal form. Why? Because the edit contact screen can become cumbersome and intimidating to many. It also can be cluttered with information a client does not need to see 99% of the time. Also, by using an Internal Form, we can set up certain levels of customizations with radio buttons and dropdown boxes that not only simplify the data entry, but also make it more uniform and accurate.

There are other less obvious but equally important reasons for using a *New Contact* internal form instead of the built in methods for creating a contact. For example, you may want to have logic that requires certain fields at a minimum to be filled out. Or, perhaps you want to trigger automation after that contact is created. By using an internal form, you can simply create an automation sequence to do whatever automation tasks you want.

I have been able to re-train many employees for clients that were supposedly incapable of learning or working with Infusionsoft, just by setting up a properly designed Internal Forms-based approach to their roles within the business. Rather than training them on the full interface of Infusionsoft - generally a mistake - we simply created a "mini-interface" with a collection of a few Internal Forms, giving them the functionality they actually needed.

This is such a simple and elegant way of running Infusionsoft in your business. It reduces it to the 20% - a perfect illustration of Pareto's Principal at work. The fact is, the vast majority of Infusionsoft users will only need access to 20% (or less) of the features anyway, so why overwhelm them with what they simply do not need?

There is one other very big benefit of using Internal Forms we haven't discussed. Using them creates automation events we can control. As an example, after a *New Contact* internal form is submitted, we can have it apply an API goal called "newcontact." Now, we can have a separate campaign that starts with that API goal, and have any business logic we want to execute attached to it.

We now have a very structured approach and our own custom events for managing our contacts.

PRO TIP: Creating custom API goals is not something you can do within the default Infusionsoft system unless you resort to the API. However, our MyFusionHelper.com app does allow you to create all of the API goals you need on the fly and use them however you want within your app. For a free trial, you can go here:

http://ismastery.com/free

After either a Note Goal or an Internal Form is used as the goal to start the campaign, you simply set up a sequence that applies and/or removes the necessary tags and establishes the required business logic.

Don't misinterpret my recommendation in this section and falsely think that I'm telling you not to use tags. On the contrary, I want you to use tags extensively in defining the business logic of your systems and processes. I merely want them to be used in a controlled fashion as part of an automated application within structured campaigns, and not just willy-nilly applied by any user within your system.

For every job there is an appropriate tool. Unfortunately, when all you can do is swing a hammer, you tend to make everything look like a nail! Tags are not the ideal thing to use in all situations. In fact, they're not even close to ideal. Nine times out of ten you are much better off using a Note Goal or an Internal Form instead and attaching the tags behind the goal in the sequences, where they belong.

Demote Yourself

By now, hopefully, you're coming around a bit to the recommendations being made in this chapter, and understand I'm not making them because I'm some kind of control freak (that's a separate discussion altogether), but out of the desire to help you create a very structured and clean system. This next concept, however, may push your buttons even more. Sorry, but it has to be said.

As humans, we like to think that we're all so unique, so different. Any very skilled and experienced salesman will tell you the opposite. He (or she) will tell you that everyone they sell to has the same fears, concerns, emotions, issues that have to be overcome, and in reality, they only really have four or five different conversations over and over and over again. The real key to being effective as a salesman is not only recognizing those situations, but being able to listen and act as if you've never heard that excuse before.

As Infusionsoft users, it is no different. We like to think that we are personally immune to all of these "junior" mistakes that everyone else makes. But the reality is we are usually the worst offenders. I'm using the word "we" here for a reason, because I'm lumping myself into this category with you. So don't think I'm just throwing you under the bus (well I am, but I'm joining you there).

At this point, you'll likely have bought into the idea of limiting and restricting your other users in your business. You'll probably agree that you could create a much cleaner, streamlined, efficient and effective system for them if you did. You'll also likely be able to envision how you could create a few Internal Forms that would really make your users Infusionsoft management roles much easier.

But are you willing to do it yourself?

Yes, that's right. I am suggesting that you limit your own usage, as well, and use the same type of structured approach you insist other members of your team use.

The way I recommend doing this, is to create a second user for yourself in Infusionsoft. 95% of the time, you'll use this secondary, restricted user. Then, every once in a while, as you need to do administrative tasks, you'll login as your admin user instead.

In the beginning, I can absolutely assure you that this will drive you nuts. I'm sorry, but it will. Because you will be using your own restricted user account and realize that you can't do what you want. When that occurs, there are two possibilities:

You can't do what you want because you need to expand the Internal Form you're using as it doesn't take one of the scenarios into account that it should, or... what you need to do is an admin-only type action.

Now, in the beginning, there will be a lot of the first scenario - that's normal. This is just part of the process. The issue is you're spoiled by always working as an Admin and you are not used to working within the system. I comes back to basic human psychology. We all like systems as long as we are imposing them on others and do not have to follow them ourselves!

So, at first, this process will drive you crazy. You'll have to do a lot of switching back and forth as you realize you need to make enhancements to what people can do within the limited access roles. But that is the blessing, not the curse. This will force you to create a very robust system that will be very powerful and usable for the other members of your team. Eating your own pie is the best way to become a good pastry chef!

The second benefit of doing this is even more powerful. And yes, even if you are a solo entrepreneur running your business by yourself with no other users in the system, I am suggesting that you should have two user roles and not be working as Admin all day. The reason is that you need to be building systems from day one. You need to be thinking about what your business will look like in six months or a year. You need to be setting it up for an outsourcing model from day one. How else can you do that unless you actually use it that way?

The fastest way to grow your business is to stop working in your business and, instead, work on your business. That means, stop doing the menial tasks you can delegate to others and, instead, focus on your core competency that allows your business to grow. We all have $10 per hour tasks and $1000 per hour tasks. Now, don't get obsessed about the actual dollar value. It is just a relative example. But all of us have things we do that make us 10x or 20x or maybe even 100x more than some of the other work we choose to do.

Right now, for me, writing this very book is an exercise for me to focus on my core values and my $1000 an hour work, instead of $10 an hour work. The real trick to growing your business is to pay others to do your $10 per hour work so you can spend more of your time doing the $1000 per hour work.

To do that with Infusionsoft, you must have appropriate systems set up and defined from the beginning. What better way to do this than to create two separate users for yourself and separate your work accordingly? You'll be creating a system each and every day that will allow you to plug in an assistant or outsourcer down the road very easily.

Setting Up Products Properly

Setting up your products properly is critical to getting valid data and reporting out of the system. This is another area I see abused due to improper usage and misunderstanding. There are two major errors I see repeated over and over again.

First, people don't understand the pricing options available with products and end up creating duplicate products for different price points, or duplicate products for different subscription plans. The fact is a single product can have multiple price points and multiple subscription plans at the same time.

A product can be both a single, one-time use product, as well as a recurring subscription product, at the same time. There is no need to create multiple products for multiple price points or multiple subscription plans.

For the subscription plan options, merely add additional plans as necessary - the interface supports multiple. In this way, you can have a $19.95 a month charter member price, a $27 a month standard member price (price increase after you moved beyond selling the charter membership) and can even add in a $69 per quarter subscription, as well as a $249 annual subscription. In fact, you could even have a lifetime one-time purchase option for $799 – all on the same product.

You can also sell a product at multiple price points without issue. The way to do this is when you place the product on an Infusionsoft order form, you override the price on the order form. The product table in Infusionsoft doesn't actually control the price charged for the product. Instead, think of it as a suggested price. In reality, however, it is on the order form that you actually control the price the customer will pay.

So, let's say that you do financial consulting and you have a product named "Financial Consulting." Sometimes, you sell a single $250 block of time. Other times, you sell it as a monthly $500 subscription. You also want to be able to sell it for a $1250 quarterly subscription, and, occasionally, you have a client for whom you want to be able to discount your $250 block to $199. No problem. All of that can be accommodated with a single product and a couple of different order forms.

Why is this important? It comes back to the "garbage in, garbage out" programming mantra. When trying to get a handle on their business, frustrated business people will often cite problems with reporting. Remember, reporting is the "end game," and that is what many use to judge how effective a system is. If the data is not setup properly, however, there is no way you'll get proper reporting.

I had a client who had a membership program they sold at several different price points over the years. They had set up each and every version of it as a different product, and the reporting was a nightmare. They had no idea of what their actual membership looked like because the data was spread out across several different combinations of products and subscriptions.

We consolidated all of this into a single product with multiple price points and multiple subscription plans. We altered existing clients subscriptions to consolidate them into the new product. We created a few different order forms and deleted others. In the end, after a lot of cleanup, we had the desired outcome. This client now has push-button revenue reporting for her membership. She knows exactly, on average, how long her members stay with her. She knows how many active subscribers she has, and she is able to run a single report and have revenue forecasts immediately available. That is why we take the time to set up products properly from the start.

The other big mistake that is made just as often with products is not setting them up into proper categories. Product categories are also trivial to set up and use. To use them, all you have to do is check a box. Setting them up is equally easy. Just "add" a new one. The problem is people just don't do it.

So why are categories so important? Categories are used extensively in the Billing Automation section of Infusionsoft when setting up triggers after a successful purchase. Depending upon how you are using purchase goals in your app (there are three different ways - E-Commerce actions, Billing Automation purchase goals or Campaign Builder purchase goals), this can be a big time saver.

By taking the time to set up the categories properly at the product level, the amount of customization needed when setting up the Billing Automation triggers is significantly reduced. It is also much cleaner and easier to follow.

Lastly, using categories allows you easier and more flexible control for promotions. When you create a promotion, yes you can do it by product, but you can also set it up by category. This can be a big time saver if your promotion spans several products that are logically organized into the same category.

PRO TIP: *This brings up a separate topic: purchase goals. As I noted above, there are actually three different methods of invoking purchase goals in Infusionsoft, and very, very few people truly understand the consequences of each method.*

Depending upon which method - or combination of methods - you use, you'll get different results. All three methods work differently. Some will not fire for manually entered purchases, for example. Some will never fire after an initial billing failure, even after it has been updated. I'm not going to go into specifics here, because these things change over time and I don't want to state something today that is immediately out of date when the next Infusionsoft update comes out.

I will, however, give you a link to an article in the Infusionsoft help desk that talks about these three methods and lays out the very distinctly different ways that they work. :

http://ismastery.com/actions

Opportunities and Sales Pipelines

Opportunities are a feature that are very underutilized by Infusionsoft users - especially the solo entrepreneur. I see that single user setups tend to think Opportunities only apply to sales teams and, therefore, do not use them. That is a big mistake and likely costing you a lot of lost sales.

Opportunities should be used by every organization that sells anything. That pretty much covers it. Seriously, though, if you're in the business of selling something, you need to track the opportunities you have to make sales. You need to have a system for following up with them. You need to have a system for documenting the opportunities and tracking them. If you do not, you are simply losing sales - I guarantee it.

A Best Practice recommendation is to create a form that is used to log new opportunities and publish it onto a very short and simple URL you'll never forget. Make all of the fields optional, even the email. The reason is, when you create an opportunity via this manual method, you want to be able to quickly get it in the system and you do not want any missing data to prevent that.

Many times, for example, you may just want to enter the name and then enter the rest later from the business card in your wallet. Or you may only have a name and a phone number, with no email, because you've set up an ad-hoc sales call. Whatever the situation, I can tell you from experience, you don't want to use required fields for this quick opportunity creation form,.

PRO TIP: *I strongly recommend you find an extremely short domain relevant to your business to use for setting up short and simple redirects. You can install Wordpress on this domain and a free plugin called, Pretty Link Lite, and use it for these types of links. Keeping them short makes it easy to use them on webinars, over the phone or, yes, even in books!* ☺

I have many domains like that. For my SaaS company, MyFusion Solutions, we have a short domain named, myfu.me - short and catchy. For my Efficient Profits business, I have a short epclix.com domain. For my personal consulting business, I use TroyB.me for the short domain. For this book, you see me using the ismastery.com domain. Again, there is a method to my madness and I do practice what I preach.

You don't just use opportunities manually, however. In your internal sales funnels, you should identify engagement points which are transitions from marketing to a sales opportunity, and you should automatically create an opportunity for that contact.

Opportunities abound throughout the daily workings of your business, and you need to train yourself to recognize and document them. In so doing, you will be multiplying the opportunity you have to make more sales. The opportunities module within Infusionsoft is very simple, and yet, very powerful, but only if you use it.

Did you know Infusionsoft has a Workflow system? It is completely customizable. You can set up the steps in the workflow, create automation engagement points for each of those steps, set up permissions, set required checklists and necessary actions for each step in the workflow system and much more. Oddly enough, they named this *workflow system* a Sales Pipeline.

That single naming choice is responsible for so many oversights in what can be done within Infusionsoft, it drives me crazy. Because it is called a Sales Pipeline, many businesses that should be using it, for their service deliverables workflow system, for example, never even consider it.

But the truth is that the Sales Pipeline is nothing more than a highly customizable and configurable workflow system. Many brick and mortar businesses are services-based and could really benefit from a workflow system to track, document and control the progression of their service deliverables. The Infusionsoft Workflow System (ok, ok, the *Sales Pipeline*) is perfect for that.

To illustrate, let's consider a website development company. After a purchase, they have a series of steps they need to walk the client through. From gaining access to the clients hosting account, to having them purchase a required theme or plugin, or any of a litany of other tasks. When I consult with a services provider like this, I see all kinds of ad-hoc systems. Usually, however, there is no system at all and the client is just "winging" it.

Imagine, instead, if there were predefined steps in a workflow. That for a client to progress from one step to the next, there was a checklist of tasks that had to be completed first. That when a client was put into one of these steps in the workflow, they were automatically notified via email of certain things they needed to know or do and the staff member managing the project was also notified of tasks that he or she needed to carry out. All of this, and much more, can be done easily within the confines of the Sales Pipeline. You just have to stop thinking of it as a Sales Pipeline, and, instead, think of it as a generic workflow system.

With Sales Pipelines, there is one last piece of Best Practice advice I want to leave you with, and it is regarding how to control automation of Pipeline Stages. Infusionsoft allows you, inside of the Campaign Builder, to create powerful and robust sales stage automations. You can create a goal type of **Moves an Opportunity** to control how contacts are moved through your workflow system / sales pipeline. This is very powerful, but also a bit dangerous.

The problem is, when someone is moved into a stage that has automation in it, that automation will automatically start and will not end unless there is an appropriate end goal. That makes sense, but it causes a lot of grief. What I see happen over and over again is clients put in automation on the "Moves Into Stage" goal type, but they neglect to put an ending goal. Then, when a contact is moved between stages, each stage they move into will start a new series of automations, but the previous stages will also continue. This creates a real mess.

There are lots of ways you can prevent the problem and I've seen many recommendations, but my Best Practice is to always use a stop goal of type "Moves Out of Stage" at the end of every Sales Pipeline automation campaign. This way, as a contact is moved from stage to stage, each time they move out, their previous stage will end.

Now, there are times when you will not want to do this, but most of the time, you will. If you have a sales stage of "Send Proposal," for example, you do not want that process to continue if you accidentally put them into that stage and immediately move them into another stage.

This brings up another Best Practice I have developed over the years of seeing many such mistakes made. I recommend you always put some sort of delay timer as the first step in the sequence of stage automation campaigns. Even if it is just a five-minute delay, it gives you the opportunity to have an "oops moment," and not suffer for it. Because stage moves are manually performed, it is just human nature that you will have some "oops" moments occasionally, and my recommendation is that you plan for them, rather than be surprised by them.

Think of this as that 5-minute send delay you can setup in Gmail so that your emails aren't immediately sent when you hit send. It just gives you a margin of error to help you not look stupid – lol.

Wrapping It Up

Like anything we do, you can just do it, or you can take the time to do it right. While "right" in the context of Infusionsoft is always a debatable topic, there are certainly "better" ways to do it. Hopefully this chapter has shown some of those to you.

Lastly, don't make the mistake of getting overwhelmed by all of the different suggestions made in this chapter. Take those that make sense for you and implement them. Those that may be more involved, ponder them for future implementation. But do take the time to plan out your application setup process rather than just "wing" it.

CHAPTER 5

Email Best Practices

"Getting them to click means training them to click!"

Infusionsoft is, first and foremost, an email marketing platform. While the marketing automation is probably the sexiest part of the platform, the truth is, having solid email marketing practices will have more to do with your success with Infusionsoft than how slick and automated your campaigns are. Remember what we've said about technology; it is only a tool.

Email marketing is all about relationships and your willingness to invest in them. It takes effort and consistent follow through to keep your list engaged, happy and spending money with you. That investment in your list, though, is really an investment in your business, and it has the highest payoff of any investment you can make. Treat your list right and they will love you. Ignore them and, well, don't be surprised if they soon forget who you are as well.

There are many steps you can take to improve the effectiveness of your list. Some of those steps are purely technical and quite easy; we'll start with those. Others are more philosophical and derivative Best Practices that my business partner, John Sanpietro, and I have developed over the years.

John is an email marketing expert, a highly sought-after copywriter, and has developed a reputation for getting big profits from small lists and has taught list building techniques for years. Most of the Best Practices we employ in our business and will discuss in this chapter come directly, or indirectly, from John.

Optimal Email Setup and Configuration

There are a few technical things you can do to improve email deliverability that are a "must." The very first one is to properly configure your SPF record for your domain.

In non-technical language, the SPF record is used to tell email service providers Infusionsoft is an authorized email sender on your behalf. What this means is, your domain is authorizing Infusionsoft to send out emails. When they see this authorization, they are less likely to think your email is phishing.

It is always tough to explain technical concepts and I often end up using another one to explain the first. Phishing is a fraudulent process where the spammer uses techniques to pose as someone he's not - an imposter - to gain access to your data.

The perfect example of phishing would be someone calling your grandma, pretending to be from the Social Security administration, and, supposedly, confirming her social security number. In reality, they are "phishing," or, rather, trying to use trickery to get her to divulge her social security number so they can steal her identity. I know all too well how this works, as this exact thing happened to my grandmother when she was in her 80's, and it took us the better part of two years to resolve.

So when you're sending email within Infusionsoft, it is not actually coming from your domain. It is really coming from Infusionsoft, but they are sending it on your behalf and, as a customer using their software, you have authorized them to do so. The from email address you will use, though, will be your own, on your domain. Hence, the discrepancy.

Now, because Infusionsoft is a trusted email service, this usually doesn't cause a problem. However, the Best Practice in the industry is to use an SPF record to specifically name Infusionsoft as an authorized sender on your behalf.

The actual SPF record resides inside your domain level settings and is something you have to alter via your domain specific registrar. There are lots of domain registrars available, but one of the largest is GoDaddy.com. However, you need to make sure and contact support for the domain registrar that you personally use, and work with them to setup the SPF record properly.

Infusionsoft has a support document that will give you all of the technical data you need regarding the SPF record. I recommend you print it out and have it in hand, as well as a link to it, so that when you're on the call to support with your domain registrar, you have all of the information they need and can even forward them the link via chat or email. Here's the link to the Infusionsoft support document:

http://ismastery.com/spf

The entire process of configuring your SPF record takes far less time to implement than it did for me to describe it here. Once you get through to the right technical person to do it for you, it is just a quick five-minute fix. It is also something you only have to do once.

Do take the time, however, to do it. In my experience, only about 20% to 30% of my clients have had this already properly setup on their own. I usually have to instruct them to do so. That's why we're kicking off this chapter with this topic. While easy, it is important and will help your overall email marketing reputation and deliverability through Infusionsoft.

Default Templates

We have talked elsewhere in the book about the importance of taking the time to setup your Branding Center properly in Infusionsoft, but this topic does need to be re-opened in this chapter. When you configure your default templates in the Branding Center, you can specify the way an email will look when you create a new one inside of the Campaign Builder and other areas of Infusionsoft. You can specify things such as the default return email address to use, fonts and logos, email signatures and even default lead-in text blocks.

These are things that, if you don't take the time to set them up properly via the Branding Center, will take you extra time every single time you write an email anywhere in the system. More importantly, however, you'll likely introduce errors along the way.

Recently Infusionsoft introduced a new mobile responsive email builder. It is a very significant improvement of the legacy builder which has become a sore spot for long time Infusionsoft users. The new mobile responsive email builder does not, however, use the Branding Center. You can (and should) still setup email templates, but they will just be saved within the email builder templates directly, not the Branding Center.

There are a couple of things that you can do and should consider when setting up your default templates. One thing that Infusionsoft does by default with the legacy email builder is add a line of "pre-text" at the top of your emails that says, "Having trouble viewing this email? Click here." This is only added via the legacy email builder and is a non-issue in the new mobile responsive email builder. Infusionsoft will add this by default, as it is intended to allow people who cannot receive HTML emails an option to click on an Infusionsoft hosted version of the email to view it.

This might have been necessary a few years ago, but, today, the percentage of people that do not have an HTML capable email reader is almost non-existent. So the Best Practice recommendation is to not use this hosted email link option. You're probably asking yourself, "But Troy, if it doesn't really hurt anything, shouldn't we just leave it alone?" The answer is no. It actually does hurt you in a pretty significant way. Let me explain.

Today more than 60% of your readers, and maybe as high as 70% or more, are reading your email on their smart phones or tablets. When you look at an email on your smart phone, you have a very limited space to view it. What you'll typically see is the from email name, the subject and the first line of text from the email. Unfortunately, what this means if you use Infusionsoft's defaults, is that the first line of text will be the "Having trouble viewing this email?" question, instead of anything relevant or meaningful to your reader.

The best course of action is to leave this block of text as a placeholder in your template, but change the actual text to something like ">> add curiosity building statement here <<" to remind you to edit it before sending out your email.

The position and size of the text that Infusionsoft uses is actually quite good. It is small text, located at the very top of the email, above even the logo. This is perfect for ensuring that it is the first line of text a mobile phone's system will see. The only real problem is it is a virtually useless call to action, instead of something meaningful.

So, put that text to work for you. Use it to drive more email engagement by adding a short curiosity building statement there instead.

Add some line of text that will compel the user to want to click on your email on their phone and open it up and read it. Do not underestimate how important this is.

Most readers today will skim their email on their cell phone first thing in the morning over coffee, or breakfast, or on their way to work. Typically, what they do is just delete 70% or more of their emails quickly right on their phone. The ones that interest them will be left, unread for now, to be read in detail when they're at their computer a little later. Only the very compelling emails that really stand out will likely be read immediately.

So the truth is, that one little introductory line of text is actually pretty important, and can have quite a bit impact on your email open rates, engagement and overall email marketing success. Don't ignore it.

One thing you should test out in your own market is what effect sending a simulated plain text email has on your open rates. What I mean by a "simulated" plain text email is an email that doesn't have any images, branding or colors. It would be formatted as simple black text on a white background, with no borders or formatting whatsoever. It would still be an HTML email, as are all emails sent through Infusionsoft's Campaign Builder (you can't send a true plain text email via Campaign Builder). However, it would appear as if it were plain text.

What we see in small business email marketing is businesses think their customers are in love with their brand and their logo. The business owners have a general belief strong branding will improve their email engagement. What we've seen, however, is sometimes it is better off for your email to slip under the radar.

When you add strong branding, your email kind of screams at your reader, "hey, look at me!" When you craft the email to be very plain and normal looking, however, it is much more nonchalant and tends to slip through their "this is a marketing email" filter.

To test this theory in your own niche, simply send some broadcast emails to your list and monitor your open rates and engagement. You will never know until you try and it will vary by market and niche, so there's no one best answer that I can give you other than to "try it out."

That is good advice, by the way, for marketing in general. The only right answer is to test out your hypothesis in your own marketing, with your own list. The words of wisdom in this book come from extensive testing over the years with dozens of niches and hundreds of clients, but at the end of the day, your niche and your list are unique. You always have to apply and test, then observe if it worked for you.

A good hybrid Best Practice approach to branded versus non-branded emails we frequently use is to mix it up. Send out all of your transactional emails - invoices, follow-up for programs and software, etc. - through traditional branded email layouts. But then, occasionally, mix it up and do a promotional email series using the simulated plain text layout.

By mixing it up, you add some curiosity to your marketing and make things different. You are training your reader to see your brand, and that is consistent, but you're switching it up occasionally, which creates intrigue and interest. This hybrid approach, used sparingly, can be quite effective.

Lastly, there is one other common Best Practice you can use in your emails. This has nothing to do with deliverability or open rates, but it can help you with efficiency and scaling your business, and it is one of the things we do in our software business. Use a from email address that automatically forwards to our help desk.

By having your sent from email address be your help desk email address, you give people a very simple way to interact with you that is scalable. I see this mistake repeated a lot, where the business owner uses a personal email address as the from email address in their business emails and marketing. Then, over time, they become completely overwhelmed by the volume of customer replies sent to them.

Having said that, most email marketing experts agree you will get higher open rates with a more personal email address. So, even though you're using a different address for the Help Desk, keep it personal. For example, Troy@yourdomain.com or TroyB@yourdomain.com as opposed to info@yourdomain.com or support@yourdomain.com.

It also becomes very difficult to swap out and re-train your list how to communicate with you. So, it is my recommendation you set this up from the beginning.

As for the help desk, there are many to use, but what we recommend and use ourselves is Zendesk. There are many reasons why we use Zendesk, and a big part of it is we also have an Infusionsoft app named MyFusion Notes that integrates Zendesk with Infusionsoft. Although it does have robust automation capabilities, the most important reason for using it is that every single help desk interaction, ticket and conversation will be stored inside of Infusionsoft, in your CRM. This way, if you ever change help desk software, you still have all of the data inside of Infusionsoft where it should be.

You can learn more about MyFusion Notes here:

http://ismastery.com/notes

One of the main reasons for recommending Zendesk is that it is super affordable. This means it is justifiable for anyone and completely within reach, even for the solo entrepreneur. Yes, I am absolutely recommending you consider having a help desk even if you are the only employee in your business.

A help desk will streamline your support efforts, make you more efficient and allow you to easily scale as you grow - so best to start with it from the beginning. It helps you create systems by defining standard responses to common questions and build out a FAQ. This means when you're ready to hire a part-time or full-time help desk representative, most of the work is already done. I would not operate a business without help desk software.

Using this technique of making your sent from email address your help desk email allows you to easily get people to engage with your business by adding lines like "Need some help? Have some questions? Just reply to this email" - it is that simple.

Strategies to Boost Engagement

The most important thing you can do to boost engagement is to have an indoctrination sequence when someone opts in. This book is not meant to be a copywriting book, and there are many out there that really go deep into this topic. One recommended book is Ryan Deiss', "The Invisible Selling Machine," which has many copywriting examples and excellent guidance on creating an indoctrination sequence.

Here's the link for your convenience:

http://ismastery.com/invisible

One of the core concepts of a proper indoctrination sequence, however, is to set proper expectations. You have to train your list. To do that, you need to start by making a commitment to them and explaining what that commitment is. Let them know how frequently you email. Let them know what to expect from you. If you do this, you can really setup your email delivery however you want and it will work, as long as you set the proper expectation and continue to deliver on that expectation.

There are those in the industry who email daily, for example. It is not the way I do things, but it can definitely work well for some people. One such person is my good friend Ben Settle. Ben has his own methodology and emails at least once a day (sometimes two or three times in a single day). But what Ben does is exactly what I am saying here... he goes out of his way to set the proper expectation. He tells you he emails daily. In fact, he even tells you this on his opt-in form - prior to you even joining his list. By setting the proper expectation from the beginning, Ben maintains very low spam complaints and has a below average optout rate from his list as well.

So take the time to let your readers and subscribers know what to expect and you'll have a much better time of it.

One of the techniques we use to boost email deliverability, and to keep the email compliance team at Infusionsoft happy with us, as well, is to really emphasize confirmed emails in our marketing. Notice I said "emphasize," and not that we only email to confirmed email addresses. We don't.

Confirmed email addresses are also called double-optin email addresses, and are strongly recommended by Infusionsoft. That being said, any time you introduce a barrier in any process, your results will be reduced. It is just simple math that if you require someone to confirm their email address with you, then you will have fewer subscribers.

It is really quite a debate on the value of an email address if that person is unwilling to confirm it, but that's not a debate I'm going to it into in this book. The fact is there are many reasons a subscriber might not confirm their email address which have nothing to do with their desire to be on your list. So, it is our recommendation you not require people to double opt-in.

There is a middle-ground option with Infusionsoft, however, that is considered to be, by many (myself included), a best practice. That is, using an optional confirmation process. The goal is to get people to confirm, but if they don't, they still remain on your list. This way, you get many confirmations, which will help your email deliverability and reputation with Infusionsoft, but you don't limit your list to confirmed emails only.

Like anything, the devil is in the details. There are a couple of different ways to implement an email confirmation process in Infusionsoft and, unfortunately, the easy method is not what I use or recommend. The simple way is to use the Infusionsoft confirmation widget in the Campaign Builder. You simply drag and drop it into you campaign and, "boom," you're ready to go.

The problem is, you have almost no control over the text in that email confirmation. It is a very rigid solution that some use, but I find to be too restrictive and limiting.

The more flexible and preferred method I use is via legacy automation links. Infusionsoft, like any software platform that has evolved and been around a few years, has some "legacy" features. Features that used to be the only way you could do things, but have now been improved or replaced. Some of those legacy features, however, have golden nuggets in them I still use extensively today. Automation links are one of them.

With a legacy automation link, you can create your own email confirmation link. You can then put that link into your email, and when someone clicks on it, they will be confirmed and also sent to an

Infusionsoft-hosted landing page that has a thin black bar across the top making it very clear they just confirmed their email address.

What most Infusionsoft users do not know, however, is that you can completely customize that Infusionsoft hosted landing page. You cannot remove it from the process, and you are required to display it per the Terms of Services of Infusionsoft - so don't go and do something outside the lines and get in trouble.

What you can do, however, is completely change the HTML of that page, adding your own branding, logo, text and signature. The black bar with white text Infusionsoft displays to draw attention to the user that they just confirmed their email address will still be displayed at the top, but you can change the rest of the look and feel of that page.

You have access to the full HTML of that confirmation page, and therein lies the next hack. You can add a simple HTML meta refresh redirect snippet of code that will allow you to redirect to another page.

WARNING: *Please pay careful attention to the exact details of what to do. If you do not heed my advice, and try to shortcut or ignore it, you will put your entire email account with Infusionsoft at risk for violation of their Terms of Service.*

Infusionsoft is very clear that you cannot try to manipulate the system. You must show their confirmation page. You can customize it, but you must show it. You must tell people in the email that contains the legacy automation link they are confirming their email address. You can't try and trick people into confirming by not disclosing it.

What you can do, and what I do in my businesses, is configure that confirmation page to be displayed for four seconds and then automatically redirect to the giveaway or PDF URL directly. This follows their Terms of Service requirement to display the page, but it also allows for an ideal user experience by quickly getting them to what they want.

So let's recap the process:

The user opts in to get a free resource from you. In the email, you send them a link and disclose clicking that link will confirm their email address with you and allow them to instantly download their free report.

When they click on the legacy automation link, it takes them to an email confirmation page on Infusionsoft that you've customized with your branding and a short message thanking them for confirming their email and telling them that they are about to be automatically redirected to the free report.

You modify that page so it displays for four seconds and then redirect to the URL where your PDF is hosted, so they can immediately gain access to it.

This is the full process I use and recommend as a Best Practice for optimizing your confirmed emails within Infusionsoft.

Don't try to cheat the system and reduce the time below four seconds. There is nothing magical about that number other than I feel it is long enough to allow them to read the short message on the page, as well as long enough to satisfy the Terms of Service requirements of Infusionsoft that you show the email confirmation. It is also short enough not to disrupt the continuity of the experience for the user.

For a demonstration video on how this works, you can go here:

http://ismastery.com/confirm

Keeping Your List Clean

Email hygiene - keeping your list clean and pruned - is an important aspect to Best Practices management of your email list. I would say less than 10% of the clients I've worked with and/or audited in the past few years have had proper email list hygiene implemented. This is a much underutilized practice, but the best marketers in the industry do a very good and proactive job of keeping their list clean.

Infusionsoft provides many of the tools you need. Sure, there are ways to improve upon what it offers, and we have some campaigns we use internally that are specifically designed to do the majority of what you need to keep on top of your list and email deliverability, however, is readily available within the default toolset.

The key feature you want to be using is called Email Status Automation, and is accessible from the **Marketing -> Settings** menu. With email status automation, you can create rules for what the system should do with all of the various types of email bounces that occur.

There are hard bounces and soft bounces. Spam blocks and email full bounces. There are far too many different statuses and types of email bounces to go into here. Besides, doing so would provide little real value.

Infusionsoft will automatically stop emailing to bounced email addresses (these are basically invalid emails), but using email status automation, you have very granular control over what to do in various situations. For example, you may want to choose to try sending to certain soft bounces three times before removing them from your list.

The Best Practice recommendation is to use a controlling tag for your marketing list(s). I always create a "Marketing" tag category, and then create separate tags for my marketing lists. I frequently have multiple lists, so I will use multiple tags under that category, as necessary. However, I will also always have at least one tag named "General Marketing List".

Using email status automation, I can then remove that tag from a contact based upon the rules I've setup regarding the various bounce types. That will prevent me from emailing that person in the future. Actually, it won't prevent me, unless I forcibly opt that person out of my list, but because I use the tag as a controlling mechanism, it does effectively accomplish the same thing.

What I mean by a "controlling mechanism" is when I send out a broadcast email, or add a series of contacts into a marketing campaign, I first filter by the presence of that "General Marketing List" tag. This way, I'm only emailing those people on my "clean" list.

Email hygiene is important because, without it, your list will become very low quality. Because of this, your reputation with email service providers such as Gmail, Yahoo and others, will suffer. Making them happy keeps your email deliverability up and your marketing efforts on track.

Some Quick Tips for Better Click Through Rates

Email open rates are nice, but, at the end of the day, what we really want is to get people to click on our emails. Yes, we want them to read them, but, usually, our emails are sending them somewhere to do something, and to get there, they need to click. Getting them to click means training them to click - it really is that simple.

Think of the experiments with Pavlov's dogs. He used training and conditioning so that whenever he rang a bell, the dogs began to salivate. Now, I'm not suggesting you become such an effective copywriter that you can have your list drooling over you, but you can certainly condition them to take action.

The easiest way to do that is with consistency and shorter email messages that don't present confusing options. There's nothing wrong with longer, newsletter style emails occasionally, but if you want to get your list used to reading your content and train them to click on your links, you need to keep your content shorter and only give them one CTA (call to action) in the email.

This is probably the second most common problem I see with client email marketing practices. The first, believe it or not, is they simply don't email their list. The second most common problem is what I call the "Newsletter Syndrome." They send out a monthly or weekly newsletter only, and nothing more. This newsletter is loaded with images, graphics and fourteen hundred links the reader can click on. Between too much color, too much content and far too many distractions, it is usually a visual assault on the senses.

Newsletter style emails have very little sex appeal - there, I said it. If you want people to read your content, be compelling, be original, be unique - BE YOU! But just creating a bland, weekly, formatted newsletter that feels cold and corporate will do very little for creating a loyal fan base.

So, instead of covering four or five different topics in a newsletter, look to create shorter and more topically focused emails that only have a single call to action. If you want them to go watch a video, make that the only action you ask them to take. Don't confuse them with links to your Status Update on Facebook and your three latest blog posts.

Train your people to read your content and to engage with it (click) by delivering shorter morsels that are easily consumed, and only ask one thing of them. If you don't believe me, make the commitment of doing this for 30 days in your business and simply test it out for yourself.

Lastly, I said that "Newsletter Syndrome" is the second biggest email marketing problem I consistently see, so let's address that first one a bit. The biggest problem is actually sending emails out in the first place.

It always amazes me that, during the client intake process, most clients are very aware of the need to grow their list. They are very in tune with how important having a list is and that spending money to grow it and acquire leads is paramount to their business growth. Those very same clients, however, are also quite reluctant to email their list.

So you spend the time, effort and money to build your list, but then ignore it? Sad, but true. This happens far too often. I'm not a psychologist, but I do observe human behavior, and I believe that this comes down to two separate issues.

The first is the technology and the feeling of overwhelm it can create. I think many people simply feel overwhelmed by the process of creating a campaign in Infusionsoft and get stuck on stupid (my not so gentle way of saying they procrastinate). The task seems to get harder and harder as they continue to "think" about it, rather than just do it.

Procrastination and overwhelm are problems of business in general, and not specific to email marketing. They are, however, very amplified for entrepreneurs. As an entrepreneur, you're on your own. No boss to look over your shoulder and no one to nag you into doing what you don't like or want to do. So developing discipline in this area is something you'll need in all forms of your business.

My advice, as curt as it is, is simply to get out of your head and just do it. I like to think of action as a muscle. Like any muscle, the more you use it, the more it grows and the easier it is. Likewise, the more action you take, the easier it gets. So just set a small goal, don't make it too difficult and get started.

Secondly, I believe many people simply are fearful about writing. Either they don't know what to say, or are fearful people won't like what they have to say. I believe this is probably a fear that was deeply entrenched in all of us back in high school, to drive your business forward, you must learn to email your list.

So, really, you have only two choices - either change your way of thinking about it and take action, or hire someone who will handle the email marketing for you. Actually, there is a third choice. You can choose to stay where you are and do nothing. It is up to you.

CHAPTER 6

The Ideal Welcome Campaign

"Set the tone to reflect how you want to be seen and positioned in your market"

Systems are predictable, stable and reliable - so why not systemize the way you welcome new users onto your list to create a more predictable, stable and reliable income stream? The fact is the *Welcome Campaign* or *Indoctrination Campaign* is the single most important campaign in your Infusionsoft app, but it has likely not been given as much thought as it should.

In this chapter, I'm going to present you with some techniques to structure your Welcome Campaign for ideal results. Some of these techniques are fairly basic and some are quite advanced. Remember, though, that this book is not about copywriting. I'm going to be telling this story with the skewed perspective of focusing on just the technical items you can do to improve the campaign. There are many other marketing books you can purchase that will help you with writing compelling and effective copy.

The Purpose of the Welcome Campaign

Most people don't really stop to think about what the purpose of their campaign is. They're working on a deadline to get it done, and quickly throw it together in order to meet that deadline. While getting things done is important, it is also important to come back and refine them. So, if you find yourself in that camp - no judgement here; you did what you had to do - but now, let's step up your game and really craft an *Ideal Welcome Campaign*.

These are the steps I take when creating an Ideal Welcome Campaign. This list is not all-encompassing or in any particular order. In some markets or niches, you will need to expand or reduce it. The important concept is not the absolute definition of this list, but the fact that I have one, and have taken the time to think about the desired outcome of the campaign before starting it.

- Introduce and position yourself in your market

- Set the expectations for email delivery and style

- Take steps to boost email deliverability

- Expose them to various channels of communication

- Track and rank their engagement by channel

- Track and rank their spending patterns

- Expose them to your core product funnel

Remember my philosophy that every campaign you build should, first and foremost, be an experiment. This is most important with your Welcome Campaign. The truth is, if you don't get things right here, subscribers won't stay on your list very long anyway, and nothing else really matters. So, having a very well structured set of metrics in your

Welcome Campaign will give you the data you need to adjust your approach over time, and refine this campaign into a well-oiled machine.

Segmentation is not mentioned in these steps because it is an assumption throughout the process. I talked about it quite a bit in Chapter 2, and segmenting your audience into its elemental avatars (or primary groups) is a critical part of your marketing. Remember, our goal is to deliver the right message, to the right person, at the right time.

You cannot get your message to the "right" person if you are not segmenting your list from the beginning. Whether you segment them before they opt in, use a survey within your initial marketing sequence, or maintain entirely different lists built from using different segment-specific lead magnets (free giveaways used to build a list), the importance of segmentation can't be overstated.

Introduce and position yourself in your market

It is important to set the tone to reflect how you want to be seen and positioned in your market. If you are positioning yourself as an expert in a given field, then you need to be prepared to back it up, or you will quickly drive people away.

The easiest way to do this is to simply demonstration and show your expertise by teaching. Client case studies and results are also very useful. This is far more effective than telling your audience what an expert you are or touting your experience, pedigree or certifications.

Set the expectations for email delivery and style

If you are positioning yourself as an occasional email marketer, but email four or five times a week, that won't resonate with your audience, and they'll unsubscribe. So set the proper expectation, and be mindful of the implied contract you're creating.

Let your readers know how often you generally email and what types of email you send out. If you always send out a Tuesday newsletter email, let them know to expect it. If you have a monthly email, with random emails in between, let them know that. Setting expectations is important so they know what to expect from you. If they're not a good fit for your list, you want them to unsub now, so you don't waste any time or effort trying to cater to the whims of people who just don't align with you.

Take steps to boost email deliverability

If your email doesn't reach their inbox, it really doesn't matter how good the content, product or service is. So, you've got to take some steps to maximize your deliverability. There are a few simple things you can do to help.

First, give them some instructions about how to whitelist your email address. This is also part of setting expectations because you can inform them that all of your emails will come from youremail@yourdomain.com or whatever email address your using.

Next, you want to deploy a great engagement tactic my business partner, John Sanpietro, teaches. It is called, "The Quick Question Email." This is an email you send out two hours after they opt in. That timing is important and has been tested. What you're doing is striking while the iron is hot and you're still very fresh on their minds.

The subject line for this email is, surprisingly enough, "Quick Question." In the body of the email, you let them know you're genuinely concerned about getting them the content that best meets their expectations. You ask them to reply back to the email and give them some guidance on how to do so.

Here's an example of the "Quick Question" email:

Subj: Quick Question

Dear (firstname),

Here at (company), we don't want to just provide you with great information. We want to provide you with the information that's <u>most</u> <u>relevant</u> to you and your business

The question is, how can we improve?

Please take a moment and reply to this email with:

- Concerns you have about (your niche)?

- What are your current struggles with (your niche)?

- What is the biggest challenge you've faced with (your niche)?

- What can we do to make sure you're gaining the knowledge you want and need?

We appreciate your time and look forward to your reply!

At this point, you're probably wondering why this is in the "boost email deliverability" section. Yes, this tactic will help with engagement, as well as building trust and rapport with your list, but it will also help with your email deliverability rate. Why? Because those who reply will be almost guaranteed to receive your future emails.

Email service providers look at email as a two-way communication channel. Many marketing emails, however, are just one-way communication. When you get the receiver to reply back to you, though, you're showing the email service providers your content is engaging and is a two-way communication. They will, in turn, boost your deliverability rates - meaning more of your emails will land in the inbox instead of the promotions tab or, even worse, spam folder.

The third suggestion to improving your email deliverability is to use the Optional Email Confirmation technique I introduced in the prior chapter. It is a known fact Infusionsoft prefers you have a confirmed email list. It is also a known fact they reward those who have confirmed email lists.

For example, a broadcast email is actually segmented into two separate lists, based upon those who are confirmed and those who are not. The confirmed emails are sent out from the top tier of email servers, while the non-confirmed are sent from other servers. In other words, confirmed emails are given preferential treatment. That means, the higher percentage of your list that is confirmed, the higher your email deliverability will be.

Expose them to various channels of communication

Today we live in a multi-channel marketing environment. Gone are the days of three channels on TV. We now have hundreds. Likewise, for you to get the maximum out of your relationship with your subscriber, you need to meet them where they are, as opposed to trying to force them to engage with you via your preferred method.

What that means is you need to embrace multiple channels of communication, such as email, your blog, PDF reports, YouTube videos, Facebook posts and more. The channels will vary depending upon your audience and your niche. For some, Instagram or Pinterest are much more important than YouTube. For other niches, Twitter is a big contender. And don't forget about the upcoming live stream technologies like Facebook Live Video and Periscope.

It is all just a bit too much, isn't it? Yes, it is. That's why I suggest you just focus on the three dominant social platforms in your niche. If you have a big Facebook and YouTube presence, for example, focus on those, plus your blog and email. This is not about trying to be all things to all people. Rather, it is about recognizing the 80/20 of your audience, and catering to what is most effective.

Beyond just exposing them to these channels, though, you want to get them to opt in via those channels. What I mean by this is, you want them to subscribe to your YouTube channel, Like your Facebook Fan Page or join your Facebook Group. The point is, you want to maximize how many marketing hooks you have into them. That way, if they unsubscribe from your email list, they will still see your retargeting ads on Facebook or your videos on YouTube. This allows you to maximize your relationship with them and, perhaps, bring them back into the fold on your email list with a future promotion.

Track and rank their engagement by channel

We now start to get into the more advanced topics of this chapter. The ones that really relate to my approach of treating this campaign as an experiment. In the previous section, we talked about exposing them to various channels of marketing. I recommend taking it one step further and tagging them by those channels, as well.

My Best Practice recommendation is to create a tag category called, "Engages With," and create tags for each of the channels of marketing you focus on. So, you might have tags that look like this:

Engages With -> YouTube

Engages With -> Facebook

Engages With -> Blog

This way, I can begin to learn from my audience by tracking their behaviors. Please note, I don't recommend or suggest that you tag them for every video or every blog post they engage with. These are just high-level, general channel tags. Don't confuse this with a segment of your list based on interest type. That would be a separate, "Interested In" category, and would contain topics relevant to your primary three or four list segments. For example:

Interested In -> DFY Services

Interested In -> DIY Projects

I hope you can begin to see the power of this type of approach to tagging your contacts. With just a handful of tags, we begin to get a very good idea of how to best reach our audience, and what they are most likely to buy. We can also combine those tags in searches within Infusionsoft to create micro-segments.

The way to apply these tags would be based upon actions the reader takes by clicking on links in your emails. So, if you have a link to a blog post in your email about how the average consumer is better off hiring a DFY (done for you) service to complete their home repair, then on that link in the email builder, you would add two tags:

Interested In -> DFY Services

Engages With -> Blog

Now, if you step back and think of your entire Welcome Campaign as a marketing experiment, you'll recognize some important takeaways. If you want to learn which type of platform your audience prefers, (for example: your blog, YouTube videos or Facebook posts) you need to construct the experiment in a scientific manner.

What I mean by that is you need to give each of those three channels an equal opportunity to get a click. So you would create, during the course of your campaign, three blog links, three Facebook links and three YouTube links spread out across nine emails. This way, you're giving each an equal weighting and an equal opportunity to get the click. Now your data will be more useful as you look at the percentages of people who engage with YouTube as compared to Facebook.

But if you only had one YouTube video link in all of your campaign emails and ten different links to Facebook posts, then you would obviously skew the data, and make the experiment null and void. Are you beginning to see what I mean when I say to craft your campaign as if it were an experiment?

This type of approach takes some thought and planning, but the data it will provide you is very telling. As an example, I had a high-end, DFY funnel client a few months back who had three primary channels for communication: a forum, Facebook and YouTube. His product was a very high-end product - the Rolls Royce of his market - and had exceptional quality, design and sex appeal.

He insisted his forum was, by far, the most popular channel he had for engaging his clients, and wanted to focus 75% of his marketing efforts there. I, on the other hand, speculated YouTube was going to be a much bigger draw, because it would showcase the quality of his product in visual detail and really make a visual impression on people. So, we set up the experiment.

The result, after several hundred people had been through the funnel, showed people engaged with the videos nearly three times as much as they engaged with the forum. The client really did not have much of a presence on YouTube, so the videos we linked to weren't even his. We just found some videos from other users of his product that were compelling to illustrate the importance of this channel. Unfortunately, despite the clear evidence, he still does not have much of a YouTube presence.

So you can craft an elegant experiment and get the data to help you market more effectively. In the end, though, you still have to be willing to learn from what people tell you. Marketing is not about YOU. It is about your audience and what they want. They vote with their wallets and they vote with their clicks, but you have to be humble enough to set aside what you want to do, and listen to them, instead. This is probably one of the worst mistakes a marketer can make - marketing to him or herself - rather than their audience.

There is no perfect length for your Welcome Campaign, and there is no perfect number of emails you should send. In general, my recommendation is a 30 to 90 day Welcome Campaign. I prefer the latter. This allows you to take the time to really "craft" your campaign and plan it out. You'll begin to lay out the number of emails necessary to conduct the experiments you want. Then, you'll combine that with your email frequency. Those variables will dictate how long your Welcome Campaign should probably be.

If it goes beyond 90-days, you may wish to examine if you're being too ambitious and trying too many experiments. Remember, the best approach is to start out fairly simple and then refine it over time. Do not make the mistake of trying to make everything perfect at the risk of never getting it done.

One last consideration when mapping out your strategy of what to email and when is email open rates and engagement will be stronger in the first few days. A subscriber will be most engaged with you then because they just joined your list and are still curious to find out what you're all about. So make sure you spread out your experiments in a way that takes that into account.

For example, if you decide to do three links each for Facebook, YouTube and your blog to gauge relative engagement between those three channels, you would not want to have the three YouTube related emails in the first 10 days of the campaign, and the blog and Facebook links later. That would skew the results to favor the YouTube links. The best approach is to rotate through the channels.

Track and rank their spending patterns

This is the most important experiment of all - how much does your average subscriber spend with you during your Welcome Campaign? This question is so simple and so fundamental to effective marketing, yet my experience shows eight out of ten business owners cannot answer it because they simply do not track it.

Today, for most businesses, an effective online paid marketing campaign is critical to rapidly growing and expanding. Without proper tracking, though, you're flying blind with your advertising budget. How can you possibly know if an advertising budget is working well if you don't have the data to back it up?

The Best Practice recommendation is to setup a custom currency field specifically for this Welcome Campaign, and track every purchase made by your subscriber while he (or she) is within the campaign. This sounds tough, but it is pretty simple. You will, however, need a plugin that extends the Infusionsoft Campaign Builder with additional math functions such as my company's MyFusion Helper app (link to free trial below).

http://ismastery.com/free

Here's how you'd make this work. First, you'll need a controlling tag to apply at the very beginning of the campaign and remove at the very end of the campaign. This controlling tag will determine whether the contact is actively within the Welcome Campaign. We need to know this because whenever a purchase is made, we will then check to see if the contact has this tag or not. If they do, we'll add the value of their purchase to the campaign custom field.

To do this, you will need to do some math inside of your campaign. This is something that Infusionsoft does not do inherently, but we use our own Math It Helper inside of MyFusion Helper.

Next, we need to setup the logic so that any purchase will be evaluated to see if it was made within the campaign or not. To do that, you need to create a Campaign Purchase goal with "Purchases Anything" specified, use a Billing Automation trigger, or use an E-Commerce action for a successful purchase. Yes, there really are three different ways you could do this, and it does depend upon how your system is configured. If you're unsure, refer to the link provided earlier in the book here:

http://ismastery.com/actions

What we are doing is creating a trigger that fires off whenever anything is purchased, and evaluating whether or not that purchase occurred while the contact was still actively in the Welcome Campaign.

The reason we need to use a custom API integration, such as MyFusion Helper, is to add the value of their last purchase to the custom field so we can track the campaign value for the contact. In order to do that, we also need to be able to reference the value of their last purchase. Again, to do that, you will need an API call. To get the value of their last purchase, we use the Get The Last Helper inside of MyFusion Helper.

To summarize, when any purchase occurs, you use the controlling tag to first determine if they are actively in the campaign. If they are, we look up the value of what they just purchased and add it to the value already stored in the custom campaign value field. That custom field becomes a running total for all of their purchases during the campaign.

Now for those of you familiar with Lifetime Customer Value (LCV) style metrics and used to storing them in custom fields within Infusionsoft, you'll likely recognize this approach. The only real difference is we're not looking at the *lifetime* customer value, but rather the *campaign* customer value. For simplicity and consistency, my Best Practice is to name this custom field, "CCV WelcomeCampaign." The CCV prefix stands for *Campaign Customer Value*.

With this structured tracking in place, you can now determine exactly how much an average lead is worth to you in your front-end Welcome Campaign. Now you will have many other marketing campaigns after this Welcome Campaign which your subscriber will traverse during their lifetime on your list. Hopefully, there will be many purchases during that lifetime. All of those purchases would be represented by a LCV (Lifetime Customer Value) calculation, a function also included in MyFusion Helper.

The goal of the Welcome Campaign (from a financial standpoint) should be to at least break even for the advertising costs invested. By tracking this CCV, you will be able to determine if your Welcome Campaign is working well or not. Let's look at an example so this all makes a bit more sense.

Let's say you are using Facebook PPC to drive traffic to a squeeze page where you give away a Free PDF report and your average lead is costing you $3.12 in Facebook advertising.

The initial goal of your Welcome Campaign would be for your average subscriber who goes through that campaign to generate at least $3.12 for you. That would mean your list building would be free, and any backend products, services or offers your subscriber purchases subsequently would be profit.

This is not the holy grail of goals by any means. This is just a measurement of an acceptable Welcome Campaign. Your goal should be to get into profitability in the first 15 to 20 days of the subscriber joining your list. You need somewhere to start, though, and you need to know what the minimum acceptable level of performance is. You can easily expand and refine the tracking in the future to report on average lead value at 15 days, 30 days, 60 days, etc.

Expose them to your core product funnel

Your core product funnel should be the focus of this Welcome Campaign. No matter what business or niche you are in, you likely have many products and services to sell. Your core product or service is the one most important to your business growth and stability.

Note that I said, "growth and stability." Those are two very different objectives. For example, you may sell a high-end, $10k training program, and making lots of sales of that program would really accelerate your growth. However, you might also have a $99 a month continuity program, and adding several of those sales each month would really help your business stability by providing consistent recurring income.

While sales of $10k at a time would provide nice revenue, they might also be more infrequent, creating ups and downs in your monthly cash flow. It might make more sense - at least until you hit a specific target income level - to focus on more reliable recurring income as your core offering.

This book is also not meant to be a lesson in how to build a funnel - there are many of those on the market as well - so I'm not going to go into a lot of detail about what this funnel should look like. However, a successful funnel will usually have various offers at various price points, and typically will escalate in value as purchases are made.

You should also, as a Best Practice, explore the use of 1-click upsells in your funnel. I highly recommend you use them as they will typically boost conversions by as much as 20%, and revenue even more. 1-Click upsells were really pioneered by Amazon.com. I'm not sure if they were officially the first to do them or not, but they certainly made the concept a mainstream marketing must-have.

A 1-Click upsell occurs immediately after someone purchases a product from you. It is shown on the very next page they go to. Since we now have their credit card on file, we can use some API magic to simply charge the next transaction to the same card they just used (with their permission, of course). On this second transaction, you do not need to ask them for their billing address or credit card details at all. You can simply ask them if they would like to upgrade their order to include your second offer, and instruct them to click the **Add to My Order** button (or whatever you choose to call it).

The reason I'm going into the whole 1-Click upsell process when I just got through telling you I wasn't going to go into much funnel marketing detail is because it is relevant to this section and your core offer. It is my Best Practice recommendation you have many offers of varying price points and types (video training versus physical product, for example), but that they all funnel, via a 1-Click upsell, to your core offer.

Let's consider this advice in more detail and imagine that you have five different products to market in this Welcome Campaign - four products, plus your core offer. Following my Best Practice approach, you would have four different offers in the funnel and each of them would employ a 1-Click upsell that would feature your core offering. Using this method, you are trying four different offers to see which one resonates with your audience, and each time they make a purchase, you're also giving them an opportunity to purchase your core offering.

By doing this, we have created 4x as many eyes on our core offering and we've done it when they are most likely to buy - after they just bought. This structure for your Welcome Campaign will invariably produce the best results for your business. In time, however, you may shift what your core offering is. My recommendation, however, is to find a mid-tier price, recurring product or service.

Strong, recurring income is the quickest way to stabilize your business. What is a mid-tier price point? That really depends on your niche. Sorry to be vague, but I have clients who sell $9.95 micro-continuity core offerings and clients who sell $2500 monthly recurring core offerings. Both are considered low- to mid-tier for their respective markets. My belief is you already know - for your market - what a mid-tier price level would be.

Bridge and Feeder Campaigns

The purpose of a bridge campaign, or feeder campaign, is to deliver a giveaway and then, perhaps, one or two emails to bridge the conversion over and then put them into the main Welcome Campaign.

What you do not want to do, though, is create ten different indoctrination campaigns just because you want to create ten different giveaways or lead magnets. This is simply not stable, and will lead to inconsistent indoctrination, as well as a lot of wasted time and effort. Instead, use the lead magnet to get the lead. Then, deliver it to them via email and use one or two emails to transition them over into the default Welcome Campaign. Using this structure will allow you to create lots of different feeder campaigns and lead magnets quickly because you'll not need to create anything other than a couple of emails.

I have created a short video to show you the campaign structure for bridge and feeder campaigns. You can watch it here:

http://ismastery.com/feeder

Advanced Engagement Scoring Strategies

Consider this section a Phase II or Phase III advanced refinement to your Welcome Campaign. In other words, if you're still working on all of the other things I've gone over in this Chapter, skip this for now and come back later. It is not my intent to overwhelm you, but to expose you to the industry Best Practices, and the great potential you have with Infusionsoft.

First off, this advice only applies to mature funnels with mature product lines. If you're just getting started, the advice in this section makes no sense. This is a very granular level of refinement.

I like to create a 0 through 5 numeric ranking scale which is objectively measured for both engagement and purchase value for my campaigns. Usually, however, it will start out as a much larger number that I then reduce down to a simple 0 to 5 scale. I do this both for engagement and for purchase value, so there are two separate custom fields involved to track these two separate values.

For those of you who are quite experienced with Infusionsoft, you may already be jumping one step ahead of me, thinking of Infusionsoft's internal Lead Scoring capabilities. You'd be on the right track as what I've described so far fits very nicely within Lead Scoring. There's just one problem. There can be only one Lead Scoring system in place, and I like to score people in the Welcome Campaign not only for their engagement, but also for their spending.

The Best Practice method for doing this is to use Lead Scoring for the engagement tracking, and use a custom solution for the spend scoring.

Another problem with using Lead Scoring is the values aren't persistent. They are transient by nature. What I want to see at the end of the Welcome Campaign is a numeric, objective measurement that defines how each contact engaged with the campaign, as well as how much they spent within the campaign. While I use Lead Scoring, I also add to it a bit. Here's what I do:

At the end of the Welcome Campaign, I run each contact through a separate scoring campaign. This campaign contains logic that looks at their Infusionsoft Lead Score value, and translates it into a numeric 0 through 5. It then stores it into a custom whole number field. I also do the same thing for their spending.

I will examine the value in the "CCV WelcomeCampaign," and then create five spending threshold buckets. For example, $1 to $99, $100 to $250, $251 to $500, $501 to $1000, and $1001+. I start at $1 because anyone who purchased nothing will get a 0 score, and I want to differentiate between no purchase at all and even a low dollar buyer. So, our scale is actually six total values - 0 to 5, inclusive.

These calculations are only performed once the contact has completed the Welcome Campaign. What I'm looking for here is metrics for how well the campaign performed. I'm not concerned with these metrics for contacts who are still actively in the campaign. Only those who have completed it.

Wrapping It Up

Just like beauty is in the eye of the beholder, there is no perfect Welcome campaign that works for every client in every niche. There are, however, elements of ideal campaigns – some of which I've presented in this chapter.

I could have easily written an entire book for this single chapter; it is that important and I have that much to say on it. So please don't take the recommendations made in this chapter as the complete and full list. With many clients we have gone much further down this rabbit hole.

The purpose, however, was to give you structure, guidance and the 80/20 approach to setting up a more effective Welcome campaign than you are perhaps using today in your business.

CHAPTER 7

Tagging Best Practices

"Tagging is as much an art, as it is a science."

Tags are the most useful, and most confusing, aspect of Infusionsoft. At their core, tags couldn't be more simplistic. There is nothing inherently difficult about creating, applying or using them. The problem, however, lies in how and when you use them. Tagging allows a granularity of information that is very powerful, but also easily abused. The problem with excessive tagging is it creates a complicated spider web of tags virtually no one knows how to interpret. As a result, no one understands them. It also means many thousands, or tens of thousands, of tags are created that slow down the performance of Infusionsoft. In fact, excessive tagging is the number one reason an app might be running slowly.

Clearly, tagging is ripe for a Best Practices guide to set some guidelines to follow. This will keep things well structured and under control, as well as easy for others to understand.

In Chapter 4, I talk about how an ideal setup would only allow one user to have access to actually create tags. If you skimmed that section, I encourage you to go back and re-examine it. Creating a document for tagging practices within your system is strongly suggested. That way, you can keep their usage consistent and well understood by everyone in the organization. Whether you choose to allow others to create tags or not, you should still document their proper use.

What you'll find in this chapter is there are recommendations and Best Practices. Tagging is as much of an art as it is a science, though, and my rules and guidelines are not 100% rigid. In fact, I have used systems that clients have setup that are 100% rigid, and I can tell you they are equally frustrating. The first concept to understand is every rule does have its logical exception. There will be cases in your usage of tags within your business and application that may fall outside the lines, and that is exactly why I recommend everyone create a tag usage document for their own organization.

The Four Commandments of Tagging

1. Never create orphaned tags

An orphaned tag is a tag that has no category. All tags should be categorized. The category gives the context of the tag usage and becomes part of the organization and documentation of the tag. There is, however, one exception to this rule. When you're doing development, you may need to create a temporary tag you'll subsequently delete. In that case, I purposely do NOT put them into a category because it reminds me that they can be deleted at any time.

You can always create a "temporary" category and put them there, but I actually find if you do that, they become permanent. Whereas, by not categorizing them, they show up right in front of you all of the time, stand out like a sore thumb and remind you to delete them.

2. Create standard categories

My list of standard categories is just that... my personal list. You may obviously modify this for your own use, but I recommend the following tag categories:

Functional - Where I put start, stop and loop tags (if used, I actually have a better system I'll explain later in the chapter)

Forms - I go into detail explaining this tagging category in Chapter 7. The "Forms" category has a listing of every Web Form you create in Infusionsoft.

Campaigns - This category is also explained in Chapter 7. This "Campaigns" category will have a listing of every campaign you create in Infusionsoft.

Marketing Lists - I use this category to segment and list out the various marketing lists I maintain. This way, when I want to send out a general broadcast email, for example, I can merely select the appropriate tag within this category.

Customer Tags - I always have a Customer Tags category that keeps both the general and specific customer tags. For example, whenever someone buys anything, I apply a generic, "Customer" tag. However, in the individual product purchase fulfillment campaigns, I'll also apply a specific tag, such as "Email Marketing 101," if they purchased my Email Marketing 101 course.

Subscription Products - This is not a literal tag named "Subscription Products". However, if I have a subscription product named "Group Coaching," I would have a category named the same. In that category, I would have tags for the subscribers, active subscribers, refunders, billing failures, etc....

I always want to be able to identify and differentiate between "subscribers" and "active subscribers." This is very important. I see this mistake being made all of the time. There is no system in place for easily tracking customers who are no longer active in your membership. Fortunately, via reporting, we can figure this out and go back and apply the tags. However, using tags for this allows us to apply logical segmenting logic in our campaigns and treat them differently.

Since a subscription-based product usually has several of these types of requirements, I lump them into a product-specific category for that subscription product.

CustomerHub/Memberium/etc. - I create a category for the subscription software I use as well. There are also certain tags I tend to create, such as identifying whether the person is setup, or has permissions to certain programs or training products, etc.... which I lump these together into this category.

Engages With - As discussed in Chapter 5, this is my engagement tracking category of tags.

Interests - As discussed in Chapter 5, this is my interests category of tags.

Email - Here I track the confirmed status, information about bounces, and other related email hygiene tags.

Other Technology or Integration - If, for example, I'm using Stealth Seminar, I'll have a "Stealth" category where I'll track tags specific to that technology. If I'm integrating with another 3rd party application or software, I'll likely do the same thing.

Welcome Campaign - I tend to have a lot of tracking going on in my Welcome Campaign. To keep things clean, I put those tags into this specific category.

3. Clean up your functional tags (or better yet, don't use them)

Functional tags are tags that serve only to perform some functional action, such as to start or to stop a campaign. If you use start and stop tags, as most users do, you need to make sure and clean up after yourself.

The most critical step is to immediately remove a start tag in the very next sequence after it is applied. If you do not, that contact will never be able to re-enter the campaign because the start tag is already applied. Likewise, if you use a stop tag, you need to have a sequence after it to remove it. When using stop tags, I also recommend removing them when a contact first enters the campaign, just to ensure they'll be able to apply them in the logic of the campaign and pull the contact out, if needed.

As you can see, there is a lot of "clean up" associated with using start and stop functional tags. This is why I don't like using them at all. I do, however, use start and stop goals extensively in my campaigns, I just don't always implement them with tags.

This is a more advanced topic, but the preferred method and Best Practice I employ in all of my own campaigns, and those that we create for our clients, is to use custom API Goals. When you use an API Goal, it is a transitory event. No tag is created, no clutter is left behind, and there is nothing you have to cleanup or remove. Simply apply the start or stop API Goal and respond appropriately.

There is no way in Infusionsoft itself, however, to create your own custom API Goals. We do this through our MyFusion Helper app, and the Goal It Helper is by far the most common Helper that we use.

Here's a link to a free trial of MyFusion Helper:

http://ismastery.com/free

We even did a case study for one of our clients, and found that 37% of their tags were completely eliminated when we switched them to using API Goals, instead of functional tags.

Another side benefit of using API Goals is it actually reduces the complexity of your campaigns. You'll find many sequences and steps are eliminated because you don't have to "Apply 1 Tag," then "Remove 1 Tag," and engage in other tag-related cleanup. So, beyond eliminating the unnecessary tags, you're also just making your campaigns shorter, cleaner and easier to follow.

4. Create Meaningful Naming Conventions

Meaningful is in the eye of the beholder, but I'm a strong supporter of using naming conventions consistently so that intent and usage are easily inferred. Rather than being fanatical about it, however, I take a pragmatic approach.

For example, because tags have categories, I don't have many prefixes or naming conventions. So, by intelligent and consistent use of appropriate categories, you can easily understand the tag usage.

However, when naming Campaigns within Infusionsoft, I do use a naming convention. I want to be able to quickly understand what type of campaign I am looking at. I also want to be able to quickly search in the campaign search window and filter my campaigns by name. So, in this case, rigid naming conventions are more pragmatic and practical. In other words, everything I do, I do for a reason.

For my list of recommended campaign naming conventions, see Chapter 9.

If you are using functional start, stop and loop tags though, I do recommend using a naming convention for those tags to make them stand out even more than just the "Functional" category they are in. I use

"START <campaign name>", "STOP <campaign name>" and "LOOP <campaign name>" as my naming convention for functional tags.

NOTE: *A looping campaign is one that restarts itself automatically after it ends; it continually loops. These are a bit more advanced, but there are several good examples of when you might want to use them.*

Sending out a weekly report every Monday, for example, could be a perfect case for a looping campaign. The most common example, of course, would be a birthday campaign.

I use another type of naming convention when using Stage Goals. If I'm tracking how a contact progresses from stage to stage within a funnel comprised of a series of different campaigns, I'll create a list of stage goals.

Stage Goals allow for very simplistic Dashboard reports that give you a quick snapshot of how your marketing funnel is working. Let's say you have a webinar funnel in place. I would likely have various stage goals for that funnel, such as:

STAGE1: Registered

STAGE2: Attended

STAGE3: Watched Replay

STAGE4: Booked Consult

STAGE5: Attended Consult

STAGE6: Qualified

STAGE7: Purchased

By creating these Stage Goals, and configuring them appropriately, we can get some very quick and meaningful tracking.

If you are paying close attention, you will realize I didn't call these Stage Goals tags. That is because I do not generally use tags to track Stage Goals. Instead, I use API Goals or other goals inside my campaigns, and I name them with the above mentioned naming convention. We will get into the details behind this in Chapter 8, when we talk more about campaign reporting and tracking Best Practices.

The Seven Types of Tags

In my usage of Infusionsoft over the past several years, I've developed my own list of tag types. They really are just logical concepts, though, because Infusionsoft makes no distinction between tags. A tag is a tag is a tag, as far as Infusionsoft is concerned. I find, however, that it is useful to think of tags in terms of what type of tag they are because it keeps you more structured in your usage of them, and helps your understanding of their purpose.

Audit Trail Tags - Examples of Audit Trail tags are my "Forms" and "Campaigns" tags. Their purpose is to create an audit trail of where someone has been and what they've done. There are other situations where you'll likely need other forms of audit trail tags in your business, as well.

Functional Tags - Functional tags serve to invoke some sort of functional event or action, such as to start or stop a campaign. There are, however, other types of functional tags. For example, if you integrate with a 3rd party appointment booking software, they will use functional tags to trigger events inside of Infusionsoft.

Campaign-Specific Tags - As I discussed in this chapter, when using campaign-specific tags, I like to group them into a category named for that campaign to keep things organized.

Engagement Tags - I've talked about engagement tags in Chapter 5 and their usage. Engagement tags are used to track what types of content and channels your contacts engage with.

Interest Tags - I also talked about interest tags and their usage in Chapter 5. Interest tags are used to track what types of topics or segmented avatars you monitor are most interesting to your audience.

Segmentation Tags - These are pretty self-explanatory, but segmentation tags are used to segment your contacts into various sub-lists. For example: dentists, hygienists and office managers.

Other Misc Tags: Debug and Purge Tags - Debug and purge tags will be discussed in detail below. A debug tag is used in the development process when you're testing things out. A purge tag is used to automatically clean up after yourself by deleting all unnecessary tags used in a campaign after a certain time threshold has expired.

Debug and Purge tags are both useful Best Practices for tagging that have not yet been adequately defined.

Debug tags are a useful concept I created. They go back to my days as a software developer. Any programmer out there is familiar with the concept of debug.print - the idea of being able to quickly output the value of a variable for testing purposes. Well, I've brought that concept to Infusionsoft, as well! It is the programmer in me. I just can't get it out. Here's how debug tags work...

First of all, they are really functional tags - just a specific case or type of functional tag. I use them to track what is going on when I'm testing out a campaign. They are implemented as start goals in the campaign. So, for example, they may fire off an email to me so I know my logic is working and the contact is entering that sequence properly. Or, I may have them send me a text message or apply a note.

They are simple tag goals in the campaign used for debugging and/or testing purposes. When I save them, I always follow the naming convention of "DEBUG <some action>." This way, I can quickly and easily track them all down and delete them prior to finalizing my campaign. By using this naming convention, and by thinking of them as an entirely different type of campaign, it helps me to keep things clean.

TIP: *What I have done recently is use our Slack It Helper in MyFusion Helper to have these messages sent directly to a channel in Slack for that particular client. I find this the easiest method of all for simple debugging, testing and notifications.*

One really cool thing you can do when using our Slack It Helper is embed a clickable link that goes straight to the edit contact screen in Infusionsoft by simply merging the contact id into the URL that you include in the Slack message. This makes it super easy to work with because, when you receive the Slack message, you can simply click on the link and open up the appropriate contact directly in Infusionsoft.

I even use the emoji's in Slack via the 'Add Reaction' feature to mark tasks as complete. I use both a red x and a green checkmark on the Slack message to signify where the item has been processed. This gives quick visual feedback and makes oversight of outsourcers trivial.

By using Slack in this manner, instead of Infusionsoft Tasks, you do not have to grant access to your system to outsourcers. This protects your list, your privacy and your financial data. You also can setup private Slack channels that only certain team members can see. Lastly, you save money because you do not have to purchase additional Infusionsoft user licenses for outsourcers.

Lastly, we have Purge Tags. These tags are not removed from the campaign. Rather, they are part of the finished product. Technically speaking, these tags are also functional tags. Again, though, their intended usage is so different, I treat them as an entirely different type of tag.

Purge tags are start goals in a campaign that trigger a tag purging process. They are designed to "clean up" the campaign, after a long delay, by removing any of the tags applied which have no permanent value. All contacts who enter the campaign would also be added into the purge sequence. The sequence would have, as its first element, a long delay timer of, say, six months. Then, after the timer completes, it would delete all of the tags applied in that campaign that didn't need to be kept permanently.

Purge tags and sequences can be very useful. They allow you to put a lot of tracking data into your campaigns that is relevant in the short term, with the knowledge you will be automatically deleting or 'purging' it sometime in the future. In this way, you can be more liberal in your tag usage, while still setting up an automatic mechanism that 'self-cleans.'

I frequently use purge tags in complex campaigns where I'm doing a lot of tagging with split testing results. Split testing data can create a ton of different tags that are relevant at the time, but not really necessary in the long term. This is a perfect illustration of the purpose and use of purge tags. Just think of them as a controlling mechanism to automatically delete non-important long term tag data.

There is a lot to take into consideration when setting up your tags, but, believe me, you'll be happy you took the time later on.

CHAPTER 8

Tracking Best Practices

"That which we track, improves..."

It is a proven phenomenon that tracking alone can create improvement. When you begin the process of tracking certain key metrics in your business, your mind will begin to fixate on them. That, in turn, leads to actions during the day that lead to improving those metrics. The result is that, just from the action of tracking, you will see improvements in your business.

This phenomenon is something Tim Ferris talks about in his book, "The 4-Hour Body." In the book, Ferris references a person who didn't change his exercise or his diet. Even so, just through consciously tracking his weight daily, he lost weight. The very act of tracking his weight kept his goals at the front of his thoughts throughout the day and he lost weight as a result of that focus. The same is true in business.

Now, I'm not proposing you just track and do nothing more - quite the contrary - but I do want you to know there is inherent value in tracking. Having said that, this section is really not about tracking high level business metrics, though that is an important subject.

This chapter is all about my 3-Step Methodology for tracking in Infusionsoft. Following this process will allow you to determine lead value and ROI by traffic source, determine every marketing channel your leads have engaged with, and allow you to determine exactly where they "converted" from a lead to a customer.

By setting up this three step system, you'll finally be able to know exactly where your money is best spent to acquire new leads and customers. You'll know which traffic sources are yielding the most ROI, which generate the most leads and which generate the best leads.

After analyzing hundreds of Infusionsoft apps for clients, I can tell you that the single biggest mistake I consistently see business owners simply do not know their numbers. Surprisingly enough, this is the case in an astounding 90% or more of the clients I have analyzed.

They may have some rough ideas about their numbers, but for the most part, they are merely assumptions of what they think they know, and not driven by cold, hard, objective data. Fewer still, less than 1%, can actually push a button and show me a report of their numbers.

To many, that is the Holy Grail of small business - to be able to have simple, push-button reporting that shows a snapshot of exactly where your business is. Guess what? You actually do have this ability right now within the capabilities of your Infusionsoft application! No extra tools are needed. No plugins. No custom reporting solutions, and no extra money or investments are required to unlock this Holy Grail of knowledge. By the time you finish reading this chapter, you will have everything you need to setup this methodology in your business TODAY.

My 3-Step Approach to Tracking

There are three individual components I use in this tracking system. I can assure you all three are necessary, though you may feel like there is overlap when you first look at it. There are lots of common questions I get when I present this approach to people, and I will address them. For now, I simply ask you fight the urge to find the flaws in the model and, instead, focus on how it works.

How did I develop this? That is one question I get a lot and I can sincerely tell you this is MY MODEL. I did not learn this from Infusionsoft, nor any other Infusionsoft trainer, industry expert or advisor. I learned it from the school of hard knocks and experience.

I can also tell you, I have a lot of experience. Before you take that as an arrogant statement, though, let me tell you my definition of experience. To me, experience is nothing more than having jacked things up many times over and lived to tell about it! In other words, experience to me is not a claim of wisdom, as much as it is a claim of survival and relentless tenacity.

I have figured this out on my own over the years of trial and error, and seeing what does and doesn't work. I have used many outside tools, tracking software solutions and embraced many other methodologies along the way, and it has all brought me back to what I am teaching you here.

It should be noted, before I dive into this, that this methodology is an Infusionsoft-centric approach. By that I mean I focus entirely on what is within Infusionsoft. I will come back at the end of the chapter and discuss how you integrate this methodology with outside traffic platforms and their own individual tracking, as well. Know that the two are complimentary, so this will not be an issue.

The reason that this system is entirely designed within Infusionsoft core features is because I want it to be applicable for everyone. I do not want to give you a solution that requires you to get some outside tracking software. Tracking is so important and so critical to the growth of your business that I want to make sure everyone who runs Infusionsoft can implement this system.

My philosophy is simple. At the end of the day, the only numbers that mean anything to me are the numbers I can produce within Infusionsoft. It does not matter whether Facebook says I should have 38 optins. If Infusionsoft tells me I have 36, I trust the latter, because those are what truly made it into my system, and that is all that really matters.

Okay, let's jump in.

Lead Sources - The First Component

If I were CEO of Infusionsoft for the day, the very first thing I would do would be to require you to provide a Lead Source on every single Web Form you ever create. It is that important. Unlike many cryptically named features, Lead Sources are properly named - they track the source of your lead, where it was originally acquired, and preserve it.

It is critical you understand that a Lead Source is only set the very first time. After that it is never overwritten or updated unless you choose to do so manually. Let's talk about a quick example to drill this point in. I want you to consider the following scenario:

You have a PDF report you give away in exchange for an opt in, and you drive traffic to it from Facebook PPC, your organic Facebook fan page, Adwords PPC and your blog. For each of those traffic sources, to track Lead Sources properly, you would have a separate Web Form in Infusionsoft each with a separate Lead Source specified.

Now, consider that someone opts in from Adwords to grab your free report. They save it off to their desktop at work and get busy and go on with the rest of the day. That evening, however, while surfing the web, they stumble onto your ad again - this time on Facebook – and, once again, they opt in and download the report because now they actually have the time to read it.

In this scenario, the lead would have traversed through two different webforms and two different Lead Sources. The way Infusionsoft works, though, is the very first time the person opted in, their Lead Source would have been set to "AdWords." The second time they opted in, through the Facebook webform, the Lead Source would not have been altered.

This is a very critical concept for you to understand because preserving this "point of first contact" is what makes the ROI reporting available via Lead Sources so valuable. Now, for those astute Infusionsoft users, you'll recognize there is one assumption to my scenario above. The assumption is the person used the same email both times.

As you know, or should know, Infusionsoft uses email addresses to determine who the contact is, and has no way of knowing two different emails used by the same person are actually the same person. So, in my scenario above, if two different emails were used, then two different contacts would have been created, each with a separate Lead Source, since they came through two different webforms.

Setting Up Your Lead Sources

Lead Sources are simple to setup. You merely go to **Marketing -> Settings -> Lead Sources** in the Infusionsoft menus. Like most things with Infusionsoft, you are basically presented with a blank canvas. That means, you need to give some thought as to how you want to use Lead Sources and spend a little time laying them out according to your needs.

Lead Sources have a category, a vendor, a medium, a message, start and end dates, and a flag as to whether or not they are active. While all of these have uses, the most commonly utilized are the Lead Source name and category. Those that are very familiar with Google's UTM tracking will recognize Infusionsoft's approach, but this methodology I'm going to teach really doesn't go that deep, and I don't want to go down that rabbit hole of geekdom. Suffice it to say, with any system, you can get 80% of the benefit with 20% of the effort, and we're focusing on the 20% here.

What is the right way to configure Lead Sources? Well, here's the thing: there is no "right way." There is only YOUR way. It really depends upon your business, and how you would want to use them. It depends upon what traffic sources you have, how you advertise and how you market your services. The single most determining factor, however, is how do you want to see the data in reports? Ask yourself that question and it will dictate how you set up Lead Sources.

Whenever someone is unsure of how to configure an "input" like this, I always start by asking them, "how do you want to measure the output?" In other words, how do you want the reports to look? If you start with the end in mind (the reporting), that will help you make the right choices regarding structures at the input side.

To make it a little easier for you, let me give you some examples.

Example 1 - A consultant who primarily gets her leads from speaking at events would likely want a category named, "Events," and a separate Lead Source for each event where she speaks. This way, she'll know which events have panned out for her in the past and which ones to avoid next year when booking her speaking schedule.

Example 2 - A blogger who primarily gets her leads from organic traffic to her blog may want to use a little "magic" available via a plugin called iTracker360. This plugin reads the keyword data people were searching on and stores that into Lead Sources. She can then optimize the topics on which she writes based on to those keywords. She'll also be able to see which keywords convert best for her.

Example 3 - An info marketer who gets his leads from a variety of online traffic sources, including Facebook PPC, Facebook Fan Pages (organic), Google Adwords, his blog and JV deals, might have a more complex setup. He might want to use separate categories for paid traffic, organic traffic and JV traffic. He could then arrange the individual Lead Sources appropriately under those categories.

Example 4 - In this last example, let's consider a service provider who gets most of her leads from three accounting firms. She has a close relationship with, and co-hosts events for, each of them. She might want to create three separate categories - one for each accounting firm - and have different Lead Sources for the individual events, as well as direct referrals underneath those categories. This way, she'd be able to report not only by event but also roll up the data to the category level of the accounting firm as well.

Hopefully, these examples make it clear to you that you have complete control and flexibility in how you configure the Lead Sources and categories. I hope you also see, by walking through these examples, you really need to start with the end in mind. In other words, think of how you want to report on the data first, and then decide how to structure it.

The Purpose of Lead Sources

Lead Sources have two separate purposes. The first is to track source of acquisition - where you acquired the lead. The second is to track ROI (return on investment). We've gone into quite a bit of detail on the acquisition side, but haven't spent much time discussing ROI yet.

Today, most small businesses are either driving a significant percentage of their revenue from online advertising, or hope to do so, but just haven't figured it out yet. Either way, online marketing in some way is likely to be part of your business. ROI tracking, however, doesn't require "online marketing." Any marketing expense can be categorized, and Lead Sources allow you to easily associate expenses with them.

This is one of those golden nuggets 80% of Infusionsoft users (maybe higher) do not realize. It is so simple, so easy and takes only five minutes of time a week if you follow my system. Yet fewer than 20% of Infusionsoft users even know about it, and of those that are familiar with it, only about 10% actually do it!

To add an expense to a Lead Source, simply go to the list of Lead Sources by navigating to **Marketing -> Settings -> Lead Sources.** Then, simply click on the individual Lead Source you want to add expenses to. At the top, you'll see two tabs - **General** and **Expenses.** Click on the **Expenses** tab. After you do, you'll see you can add recurring expenses or one-time expenses.

I have to be honest. I rarely use the monthly recurring expenses, but that's just because it doesn't really fit into the way I do advertising. Most of my advertising expenses are one-time expenses or, even if they are recurring (such as weekly Facebook advertising expenses), are inconsistent amounts which still need to be treated as a one-time expense. However, if you have a monthly recurring expense, you can set it up here, and Infusionsoft will automatically add it in for you each month.

As I mentioned, my system for adding expenses is very simple and only takes about five minutes a week of your time. Each and every Monday, I log into my various traffic sources and look at their "Last 7

Day" spend report. I then copy that number and paste it into Infusionsoft as an expense for that Lead Source.

I do most of my paid advertising on Facebook PPC, so I don't have a ton of different traffic sources to cycle through. Even if you did, though, the amount of time needed to do this expense tracking is trivial, but you have to do it!

Remember the old programmer's mantra, "garbage in, garbage out." This means if you put garbage data (or no data) in, don't expect the system to be able to give you beautiful and meaningful reports. Ironically, I find that even though Infusionsoft is a systems-based tool that automates your marketing, you still have to be systemized in your usage of it, as well. Sorry, but you cannot escape personal accountability with technology (though many try).

My recommendation is to outsource this to an assistant so it gets done every week consistently. Knowing your numbers and knowing they are accurate is so vital to your business and marketing, you simply cannot afford to not do it.

Doing this one thing can radically transform your business. It is so empowering to be able to run a simple Lead Source ROI report and see what is and what is not working. The insights you'll gain from this can double or triple your business growth in a few short months.

How to Add Lead Sources to a Webform

This is a very straightforward process, and only takes one minute to implement. You simply add a hidden field to your webform. Then, you configure that hidden field to connect it to the Lead Source field, and select the value (individual Lead Source) to assign it. It essentially becomes a hidden, hard-coded value you are adding to your webform.

If you are deploying your webform via HTML to a developer to put on your website, make sure they do not strip out the hidden Lead Source values. The best practice here is to only give them the unstyled HTML, and tell them they cannot modify it at all. They can only style it. That means they can embed it onto the site and make it look however they want with CSS and formatting, but they can't remove any of the form variables.

Make sure to test your webforms to confirm they are setting the Lead Sources properly. This is super easy to do. Simply create a throwaway email address and opt in using that email address to the webform you want to test. Then, go look at the contact in Infusionsoft and make sure that the Lead Source is set properly.

PRO TIP: *For testing emails with Infusionsoft, create a Google Gmail account. Gmail allows you to take one email address and create unlimited aliases to it using a simple little trick. Let's say your email address is mytestemail@gmail.com (that's not my valid email, so don't try using it).*

Well, you could create an alias like this, mytestemail+test1@gmail.com, and it would work just fine. You can add the "+XXX" right before the @gmail.com portion of the email with any text you like and Gmail will automatically treat that as an alias to your primary email. This is very useful in testing Lead Sources because, if you recall, Lead Sources are only set the very first time they are used, after that, they won't be updated.

A curious insight about my own use of Lead Sources

I love doing speaking appearances. It probably goes back to the first time I spoke publicly on stage. It was in Brasil. I was 16 years old and speaking in Portuguese, which I had only just learned in the past three months. It was at a national Rotary convention in Sao Paulo, in front of around 2,000 attendees, as well as my other exchange student peers behind me on stage.

I know many hate public speaking and have an innate fear of it - but for me, it was love at first speach. Since then, I've given hundreds of speeches at conventions, events, seminars, and many hundreds of webinars. So, when asked by a colleague to speak at their upcoming event, I almost always have said "yes."

It was not until I started tracking those events as Lead Sources, however, and tracking the leads I acquired from those events that I realized just how big an impact it had had on my business. What I realized - and what the numbers showed me - was that I had never made less than $35,000 from speaking at an event, even though I was not paid to speak, didn't sell anything from the front or back of the stage, and had to pay my own travel and meal expenses.

How? Because I have consistently acquired strong leads that have turned into very solid business for me over time. Part of this formula for me is also that I tend to sell higher ticket consulting and services, so it doesn't take a lot of sales to make that $35k - sometimes only one sale. Also interesting to note, is that for me, that income might come as much as 18 to 24 months after the original event.

Today when I speak at an event, I always have some form of lead generation (a report, a tool, a bonus, the slides from my presentation, etc.), and I tie that to an optin with a Lead Source. I also add my trip expenses for the flight, the hotel and the meals and entertainment. With those two small steps, I can now accurately track how effective the event was for me over time.

Lead Sources Wrap Up

There are two purposes of Lead Sources - to track lead acquisition and ROI. Both require you to do your part, however, in order for Infusionsoft to do the heavy lifting. To track the lead acquisition, you must install Lead Sources on every webform in your application. To be able to generate accurate ROI reports, you must enter your expenses. It is that simple.

Tags - The Second Component

Tags, as used in this context, provide the "audit trail" of your contacts progression through your marketing funnels, webforms and campaigns. By utilizing the very simple process I'm going to show you, you'll be able to see exactly what webforms your contacts have opted in through, as well as which campaigns they have progressed through, and easily search for both.

Before I go into the reasons why you should use this approach, I just want to show it to you. It is extremely simple and only adds about five minutes to your campaign building efforts.

The first thing you want to do is create two tag categories in your app, which you will use repeatedly.

Create a tag category named "Forms"

Create a tag category named "Campaigns"

After every webform in every campaign you build, create a tag with the name of that webform and save it in the "Forms" category. Apply it to every contact who opts in through the webform.

In every campaign you build in your app, create a tag with the name of the campaign and save it in the "Campaigns" category. Apply it to every contact who enters the campaign.

That's it - it is that simple. We will then use these two simple categories, and the associated tags created therein, to establish an audit trail of where and what your contact has done. We'll be able to see every single webform they've submitted, and we'll be able to see which marketing and fulfillment campaigns they've gone through.

Now, for the objections.

Yes, I know that you can go to a contact in Infusionsoft and look up the campaigns that contact is in. I also know you can see the webform submission history on the contact record. So why am I instructing you to repeat this data in tags?

The fact is, while you can access the data, it is only visible through **Marketing -> Reports -> Campaign Contacts** and **Marketing -> Reports -> Web Form Tracking Report**, and not easily used within Campaign Builder. The data is there, but I find it much more convenient to have that data directly visible on the contact record. You'll be able to easily look at a contact and see at a glance where they have been.

By storing the data in tags, you will also be able to use that data in other, more useful, ways. Tag data gives you the ability to create automation logic within your campaigns, add decision diamonds and create inclusion or exclusion logic.

Of the three components of my tracking model, some may consider this one to be optional. Still, I both use and recommend it.

Referral Partner Links - The Third Component

The single most underutilized tracking gem provided free of charge with Infusionsoft is the Referral Partner module. This approach typically creates a lot of questions and objections, but please allow me to explain how to do it first, and then we'll talk about the objections I hear... and why they are not worth worrying about.

The purpose of using Referral Partner tracking in my methodology is to show you what marketing pieces are converting for you. So, to recap the three components of the model: Lead Sources provide acquisition and ROI data, Tags create the audit trail and Referral Partner tracking links show your conversions.

Before we talk about how I use Referral Partner tracking, it is important to understand how it was designed to be used, and why it was created. I'm obviously using it for a purpose other than it was intended (well, only slightly), so I want you to understand its higher purpose.

Referral Partner tracking is more commonly known as Affiliate tracking. If you sell your products and services, and want to pay an affiliate commission to people who send you traffic and sales, you would use the Referral Partner module in Infusionsoft.

The Referral Partner module allows you to setup commission payout structures for your products and services. It is extremely flexible and allows you to setup default payout amounts as well as create overrides. It has a ton of very flexible and customizable logic for payouts at multiple levels of referrals, as well as fixed payouts versus percentage payouts. It also gives you the control to make one-time or recurring payouts for recurring subscription products and services.

The Referral Partner tracking in Infusionsoft is very flexible and one of the best in the industry. It also includes a separate interface for the Referral Partner to login and see their commissions, ad copy and banners, create their own tracking links and much more. It is this flexibility I leverage in my best practices three-step tracking methodology.

A Quick Example

An important thing for you to understand is that, by default, the last person to make a referral would get credit for the sale. For example, let's say that two different referral partners both send an email marketing your product to their list and Joe is a contact on both of their lists.

Joe sees your product marketed by both referral partners and clicks on both of their referral partner tracking links. Later, Joe decides to purchase your product, but he clicked on links from two different referral partners. Who will get credit for the sale?

By default, the last referral partner link clicked on will be credited with the sale. Now, this is something you can override in the **CRM -> Settings -> Referral Partner Defaults** section of Infusionsoft, but, for this system to work properly, you will need to leave it as "Latest Referring" (its default value). You should confirm it is set that way.

This is absolutely critical because, for our purposes, we want to know what marketing piece the contact clicked on that led to the sale. If the "First referring" option is the selected tracking method, your data will be meaningless.

The Way We Use Referral Partner Links in Tracking

Before we get down to the down and dirty details, let's first start with the conceptual approach we're going to use and make sure you understand it. Leveraging Infusionsoft's built-in Referral Partner module, we're going to create an internal tracking system.

We will create tracking links for all of our products. More importantly, we'll also create tracking links for our marketing pieces that drive traffic to those products. In doing so, we'll be able to see which was the last link they clicked on prior to purchasing. That will provide us valuable data on which of our marketing pieces are leading to sales and which are not.

To illustrate this, let's assume you have a four-part email marketing campaign promoting a single product. In each of the four emails, you give some information and end with a call to action (CTA) link that takes them to the order page.

To improve your campaign, you first need to understand which of the emails are working, and which are not. So, we'd have different links for each of those four emails that would all send to the same product order page, but track independently. This way we could determine which emails were working well and which weren't. We'd then be able to improve the poor performers via split testing or other means.

Setting Up the Referral Partner Links

In order to use this component of my system, it is imperative you become familiar with the Referral Partner Center. As a Best Practices guide, the purpose of this book is to show you the best ways to utilize the systems that make up Infusionsoft, which will allow you to rapidly grow and scale your business. This book is not, however, intended to be a step-by-step teaching aid for Infusionsoft itself. There are lots of books like that already available on the market. Also, do not underestimate the value of Infusionsoft's online documentation available at:

http://help.infusionsoft.com

I do not believe in wasting time or effort redoing what someone else has already done. In fact, the name of one of my three businesses is Efficient Profits. That should tell you the value I place on efficiency. I did not want to write a book that simply rehashed what others do. For that reason, and to make sure this book doesn't stretch to 700 pages, I have to make some assumptions.

I am assuming you already know how to use the Referral Partner Center. If you do not, I suggest you spend some time on Infusionsoft's online help (link referenced above) and get familiar with it. In this particular case, I am also going to give you a link to a free video training resource I've created. It gives a quick overview of the Referral Partner Center and shows you how to use it in accordance with my tracking methodology. You can reference it here:

http://ismastery.com/tracking

Now we need to get things setup properly with the Referral Partner link tracking. Here's a step-by-step guide to walk you through it:

1. Set up a contact you will use for tracking as a referral partner.

My recommendation is creating a new contact named "Internal Tracking." Yes, I literally use that as the first and last names of the contact. It is not even necessary to enter an email address or other field data.

2. Set up a new commission program.

You'll likely already have a commission program set up, and it is probably named "Standard Commission Program." I want you to ignore that and create a second commission program named "Internal Tracking."

To do so, go to **CRM -> Referral Partners**. Then, from the Referral Partners menu, go to **Referral Partners -> Commission Programs**. Next, click the **Add A Commission Program** green button at the top right. Name the commission program and set the priority to 9999. I'm not going to go into too much detail here about the priority, but suffice it to say if a product is in two commission programs, and the contact is already enrolled in both, the priority will determine which one gets the commission.

If you are using the Referral Partner (affiliate) system with external affiliates, then you will want to take care that you do not create a system where you end up stealing commissions from your affiliates. The easiest way to do this is to simply create a second, internal sales page separate from what your affiliates use. I find most Infusionsoft clients are not even using the referral partner system at all, so it is really a non-issue 90% of the time and that is why I include it here.

3. Create an actual Referral Partner.

We created the contact to be used, but we haven't actually created the Referral Partner yet. To do so, go to the **Referral Partners -> Add a Referral Partner** menu link. In the contact box, simply type in "internal tracking," and it will locate the contact you've already created in step #1. At this point, you need to fill out the rest of the fields.

For the **Name**, I recommend you again use "Internal Tracking. " For the **Code**, I'd recommend something very short, such as "int" for internal. This code will be used in the links themselves, so you want it to be short and sweet and contain no spaces or capitalization. Set the **Password** to whatever you want (something secure) and set the status to "Active."

4. Notifications and Tracking

It is not necessary to set the **Notify On Lead** or the **Notify On Sale** radio buttons. The next section is the **Track leads for x days** section, and I recommend you leave it as 0, for unlimited (the default value). Lastly, just ignore the **Cart Skin** option.

You have now set up an internal tracking contact - well, mostly. Unfortunately, there is one more step, and it is a step many forget. Forgetting this makes everything else useless, so please pay attention. After you create the Referral Partner, you now have to add them into a commission program. You'll see this as a drop down box, and it is pretty straightforward. Select the "Internal Tracking" commission program and click the **Add** button at the right. Then, save the referral partner record.

That's it.

Creating the Product Tracking Links

Now, to use it effectively, you need to create tracking links for each of your products you wish to track sales for. You do that by going to the

Referral Partners -> Referral Tracking Links menu item, and adding a referral tracking link via the green button in the upper right.

When setting these up, for the **Name**, use the product name with spaces and capitalization as normal. For the **Code**, however, use a very short name with lowercase characters only, and no spaces. Again, the code will be used in the link itself and you want it to be short and sweet.

You do NOT need to specify the **Referral Partner** (that is only used for overrides), but you do need to make sure it is associated with only the **Internal Tracking** commission program by selecting it from the Programs drop down box. Make sure you don't have multiple programs selected.

Then, simply repeat the process for any products you wish to track.

Creating Individual Marketing Piece Tracking Codes

We're almost done, but we have to bring all of this down one more level to the individual marketing tracking pieces. I know I've used that generic wording a few times now without defining it, so what do I mean when I say *marketing pieces?*

A marketing piece could be any number of things, from a simple email, to a PDF giveaway, to a link in a blog post or even a radio or TV advertisement. It is, literally, any specific piece of marketing material which can lead to a sale, and where a link can be embedded.

PRO TIP: *Yes, you can embed a link into a radio ad or TV ad. You would do that through the creative use of a CTA domain. A CTA domain is a domain name (not your primary domain) that is very short and memorable. For example, as a Chiropractor, you're doing a radio spot for a free massage in your office in the month of May. You might have a domain, such as FreeMayMassage.com, and its sole purpose would be to track your traffic by* setting a Referral Partner Link which redirects to a landing page on your main site where they can book the massage.

This type of CTA domain redirect is also very powerful in traditional offline marketing that you want to still track results for. You can use it in Newspaper ads, radio ads, tv ads, flyers and pamphlets, business cards, or podcasting. CTA domains are one of the most powerful ways to track ad effectiveness.

If you would like to see a short tutorial on how to use CTA domains, go here:

http://ismastery.com/cta

If you have not watched it already, and are not already familiar with the Referral Partner Center, I recommend you put the book down for a minute and go watch this short video overview (below) about creating tracking links. I will go over it here briefly, but it is much easier to watch the video for this than to read it.

http://ismastery.com/tracking

First, log into the Referral Partner Center as your Internal Tracking referral partner. Next, click on the **Link Generator** menu item at the left. The link generator will allow you to create ad tracking links for your products.

Let's take a step back for a minute, and go back to the earlier example of a four-part email series promoting an individual product. In that example, we would need four different ad tracking links, one for each email. So, we'd go into the **Referral Partner Center**, then to the **Link Generator**, and add four new ads under the **My Ads** section near the bottom.

Again, these ad codes will become part of the link. For this reason, I like to keep them very short, lowercase text only and no spaces. For this example, I'd create four ads, such as: em1, em2, em3 and em4.

After I've created the ads, I can now use the **Link Generator** to create (generate) a full tracking link that will be specific to this commission program, this referral partner, this product, and, yes, this particular marketing piece (ad). A complete link will look like this:

http://app.isrefer.com/go/productcode/referralpartnercode/adtrackingcode

To further illustrate, let's say the product you're promoting is the Free Massage, and you setup the referral tracking link code to be "fmsg." Let's also assume you used my earlier suggested name for the Internal Tracking referral partner code of "int" and "em1" for the first ad tracking code. In that case, your link would look like this:

http://app.isrefer.com/go/fmsg/int/em1

NOTE: the "app" in the above URL refers to the name of your Infusionsoft app. If you're not sure what that is, simply log into Infusionsoft and look at the URL in your browser. It will begin with XXX.infusionsoft.com and that XXX is your app name.

To complete the example, you'd have four separate emails in your marketing sequence advertising your free massage. Each one of them would have its own unique link as defined with the structure above. When you sent out your emails, each and every click would be tracked through your custom links, and you'd be able to see all of that history in the **Link Tracking Stats** section of the **Referral Partner Center**. In this particular example, we were giving away a free massage and not selling a product, so we would only have click data.

In the **Link Tracking Stats** section of the **Referral Partner Center**, you'll be able to see all of the data showing the redirect, the ad, the hits (impressions), the opt ins created, the orders generated, the subscriptions generated, hits per order metrics, and hits per subscription metrics. You'll also be able to filter this data by date.

You'll see some ancillary side benefits, as well, such as income generated from other products as a result of your marketing efforts. It is very common you send someone to one promo and they don't buy, but they see something else on your site and end up buying that.

I just covered a simple four email marketing sequence as an example of how you might use this, but the reality is, the sky is the limit. You can use this on your website to see which blog posts are getting you the most traction, or to see if the link to your product in the navigation bar is working as well as the link in your sidebar. The ways you can use this simple process could be an entire book in and of itself!

Just spend some time thinking through it. Remember my mantra, start with the end in mind. What do you want to get out of it? What reports do you want to be able to see? Use that to guide how you use these conversion tracking links.

Advanced Tracking Recommendations

As you saw above, the links generated by Infusionsoft are very powerful, but they are also very long, cumbersome and, for lack of a better word, ugly. In fact, seeing the links themselves can actually hurt your conversions in paid advertising, and many sites will not allow you to directly publish affiliate links.

So, what do you do? Simple. You use a link cloaker. Don't let the geekspeak confuse you. This is a very simple and freely available tool which simply redirects one link to another. The easiest to use and freely available option I recommend is a WordPress plugin named Pretty Link

Lite. If you're using WordPress on your main site, simply install this plugin. It is a very lightweight plugin, and not likely to cause any conflicts with others. I would recommend just putting it in your main WordPress installation. However, if you don't use WordPress, you can always create a subdomain like "go.mysite.com," install WordPress in that "go" subdomain, and install Pretty Link Lite there instead.

What this allows you to do is create a "pretty" link on your main domain name which simply redirects to the ugly Infusionsoft referral partner tracking link which, in turn, will redirect to the actual sales page for the product. By putting this link cloaker in front of the Infusionsoft links, you can now use very nice looking links in your ads on Facebook and other places that look like they're just going to your site. The reality is, they are just going to your site, but they just have to redirect through the tracking software first.

Here is a short video showing you how quick and easy it is to do:

http://ismastery.com/pretty

Go back and read my earlier tip about using a CTA domain. This is very helpful when you're speaking on stage, for example, and you can just tell people to go to your domain. Again, a CTA domain is NOT your primary site. It is a short and clever domain name used simply to track where they came from by redirecting it to the referral tracking link. Domain redirects are something you need to configure at your domain registrar (like GoDaddy.com for example), so that when someone goes to the CTA domain, it simply redirects them or forwards them on.

Thoughts On Integration with Facebook and Adwords

When you're running paid traffic on Facebook, Adwords or any of the other big marketing platforms, tracking always becomes a little bit more complicated. Each of these platforms will have its own tracking tools which will usually involve setting a conversion tracking pixel.

So, if they already have tracking built in, why do I want to use Infusionsoft's? First, going back to my earlier statement in the beginning of the chapter, the only numbers that really are accurate are the numbers in Infusionsoft. No other source can accurately tell you how many sales or leads you generated. All of the others are only about 90% accurate (at best).

There's an even more important reason you want to use both, though. The goal and granularity of the tracking is very different. The goal of Infusionsoft tracking is to answer the high-level question of "which traffic sources are ROI'ing better for me?" However, the goal of Facebook tracking, for example, might be, "which ad set is performing the best for this marketing campaign?"

In other words, it has to do with granularity. The traffic partners internal tracking is very useful, and should be used. We also use Facebook pixel tracking to tell us which campaigns are working best, and we certainly would not want to create a Lead Source for every single short-lived ad set we create in Facebook.

So, in the end, it is about using the right tool for the right job. With Facebook or Adwords, the pixel tracking is useful for refinement of the marketing campaign and improving your results. Then, we just summarize that data in a less granular level within Infusionsoft to get down to the ROI by traffic source.

Bringing It All Together

So, to wrap up this (long) chapter, let's tie this all together.

You start your tracking with Lead Sources. These will tell you where your traffic is coming from and what the ROI of those traffic sources is. You follow that up with Tagging in order to see the full audit trail of where your contact has engaged with you and your marketing. Lastly, you use Referral Partner tracking links to see exactly which marketing pieces are converting leads into sales. That's all there is to it.

CHAPTER 9

Campaign Building Best Practices

"It is not just about what you can do, but what you should do in order for others to easily understand"

The single most powerful and misunderstood tool in the Infusionsoft arsenal is the Campaign Builder. Campaigns are the core knowledge you must become very good at in order to master Infusionsoft automation marketing.

Campaign Builder Best Practices - Core Elements

While there are technically other areas in the app that could qualify as automation, Campaign Builder is where all of your automation logic should reside. In fact, that is a Best Practice you should be following. Avoid putting a lot of logic into areas outside of the Campaign Builder, such as Action Sets. Instead, use outside Action Sets and/or global actions (such as the global action that is triggered when someone opts out) to trigger campaigns inside the Campaign Builder.

By keeping all (or at least the vast majority) of your automation logic inside of the Campaign Builder, it will help you create more self-documenting systems, will be easier to follow for others, and easier for you to maintain over time. When you start putting logic all over the app, if it is not thoroughly documented, it can easily become a spider web of disorganized code that is very difficult to follow and understand.

1. Keep The Logic in Campaign Builder

Just because you can do something doesn't mean you should. It is my strong advice you keep all of your logic inside of Campaign Builder, and use outside logic only as necessary, and to trigger off campaigns where the bulk of your logic resides. For example, let's say you need to use an action set for one reason or another.

Instead of putting a lot of logic inside the action set, have it simply invoke a campaign, and put the logic there instead. Then, inside the campaign, use a campaign note to explain this particular campaign has a dependency on the action set, and name the referenced action set by name and id. This makes things very clear.

Which brings us to the second Best Practice of campaign building.

2. Create Self-Documenting Campaigns

Campaign Builder has a notes tool built right in. Even though it should be obvious, I state that because in more than 90% of the apps I review, no one seems to use the notes tool. My only rational conclusion is no one knows it exists. It can't possibly be that people are too rushed or lazy to use it, right?

Okay, a little sarcasm, I know... but sometimes you just have to call out the pink elephant in the room, and you can't afford to be lazy or in a rush when it comes to defining business logic. That is exactly what Campaign Builder is and what it creates - your core business logic. It defines what happens when a sale is made, what happens when a refund is requested, how your sales pipeline is managed - Campaign Builder is your core business logic. If you let that set in for a minute, I hope it will become painfully obvious you have to do a very good job of documenting it.

When it comes to documentation, I believe less is better, but that doesn't mean documentation is not necessary. It absolutely is. The Best Practice methodology I teach regarding Campaign Builder documentation is threefold:

1. Name your campaigns using a consistent naming convention

2. Name the elements of those campaigns descriptively

3. Document each campaign and/or sequence using the built in Notes feature

If you follow the above three-step process, your campaigns will become self-documented and easy to follow – you do not need a formal 30-page procedural document! Let's go through each of those three guidelines with a little detail to illustrate further.

Campaign Naming Convention

It is not imperative you use my naming convention. I have seen many different naming conventions, and all are equally effective, as long as they are used consistently. That is the real key to success here. You have to actually use the naming convention you create.

I use a two letter prefix, followed by a dash, for all of my campaigns. This two letter prefix allows me to quickly determine what type of campaign I'm working with. Then, the name of the campaign tells me the rest. Here are the common prefixes I use:

MK -> Marketing Campaign

FF -> Fulfillment (post sale delivery) Campaign

RP -> Reporting Campaign

PG -> Purge Campaign

SL -> Sales Campaign

SP -> Sales Pipeline Campaign

IT -> Internal Campaign

I do, however, also create additional prefixes on the fly for different clients, depending upon the integrations they use. So, for example, if the client is also using our MyFusion Notes app to integrate with Zendesk's helpdesk software, and has Zendesk automation campaigns, I would implement those as follows:

ZD - Zendesk Triggered Campaign

Or, if they're integrating with a third-party legacy forum software like vBulletin (not a great one to try and integrate with Infusionsoft, by the way), I would use:

VB - vBulletin Triggered Campaign

The point is you will have your own internal Campaign Builder naming conventions, but you'll also have to likely expand that list as you integrate with other software solutions. The most important part is to use the conventions you standardize on.

To explore MyFusion Notes for yourself, you can check it out here:

http://ismastery.com/notes

Name Campaign Elements Descriptively

Naming your campaigns clearly is the first step, but you also need to take the time to properly name the elements within a campaign. My Best Practice and no-nonsense approach to this is very simple - provide useful and descriptive names for the elements.

There is nothing more annoying than opening up a campaign someone else created and seeing elements like "Webform" and "untitled sequence." Really? You can do better than that. This is your core business logic and you need to take it seriously. Take the two minutes necessary to actually provide some useful names for the elements so people using these campaigns do not have to try and guess what the heck their purpose is.

Name each element very purposely and descriptively. If it takes a couple of lines of text, no problem. You can use carriage returns to make the text wrap to the next line. Be clear and effective in your naming, but be as short as possible. In other words, do not write a paragraph. Just write a clear, concise name. If the situation warrants more explanation, then see the third guideline and create a campaign note.

Use Campaign Notes Liberally

The built in notes feature in Campaign Builder is very easy and effective for creating additional campaign documentation. It allows you to drop an HTML widget on the canvas and type in whatever HTML you want.

Since it is HTML, that means that you can make things bold, add headings, add colors, and, even, add external links and videos. I use robust notes when I develop campaigns for clients because it makes them very easy to follow and understand. Here are a few of the things I do using notes to make campaigns very clear.

I like to add a note called "INSTRUCTIONS" that clearly lays out how to use the campaign. If there are elements in the campaign which need to be implemented by the client or completed prior to publishing, I will use HTML in the note to make the note red. You can do this easily by using the following HTML:

```
<font color="red">your text</font>
```

If there are multiple instructions, I label them with a number, so they're easily understood as "Step #1" and "Step #2." Little stuff like this really goes a long way to making your campaigns readable.

Lastly, if necessary, I will add a short overview video, via YouTube, that explains how the campaign works. I will create a ScreenFlow video (you can use Camtasia or other software, if you want) of the campaign instructions and overview, and then publish it straight to YouTube with the *unlisted* option.

The *unlisted* option in YouTube allows you to create a video that is live and published, but also hidden. The only way someone can get to it is if they have the link for it. Be aware, though, while it is hidden, it does not have any inherent protection or privacy. It should not have any private data or client information in it, as it, technically, could get shared. If you need to make the video private, I suggest putting it behind a membership site instead.

TIP: You can use a tool like TextExpander for Mac for easily creating rich text markup boxes for your notes. For example, I use a blue box around my notes for general notes and a red box for those that are incomplete or critical.

Here is a brief video that will show you how easy TextExpander makes this:

http://ismastery.com/textexpander

Here is the HTML code I use for creating a blue border around my notes with a nice shaded blue interior:

```
<div style="border: 4px dashed; border-color:
#1980ee; background-color: #e1edf6; text-align:
left;padding: 10px;">NOTE GOES HERE</div>
```

And here is the HTML code I use for creating a nice red notes box:

```
<div style="border: 4px dashed; border-color:
#c60000; background-color: #fbc9c9; text-align:
left;padding: 10px;">NOTE GOES HERE</div>
```

3. Separate Campaigns by Purpose

As you saw in my naming conventions, I recommend separating campaigns by their purpose. For example, I have separate campaigns for marketing and fulfillment. You can combine this into one campaign, if you wanted to, but I do not recommend it.

Let's say you're selling a $97 product on website design, and you are creating your first giveaway-based marketing funnel for that product. Your giveaway is titled "7 Rookie Website Design Mistakes You Can't Afford to Make." This is all new, so you start to build out the campaign, and it looks something like this:

You have a web form to collect the lead. You then send them to a marketing sequence, followed by a purchase goal. After the purchase goal, you have a fulfillment sequence which sends them the product they purchase, as well as some follow up emails. You name the campaign "Website Design Product."

That is how 99% of Infusionsoft users would create this campaign. I, however, would have two separate campaigns. The first would have the web form, followed by a marketing sequence which terminates with a purchase goal. It would be named something like "MK - 7 Rookie Mistakes PDF."

Then, I would create a second campaign that would start with a purchase goal, followed by a fulfillment sequence. I would title this campaign "FF - Website Design Product."

For illustration purposes, both of these examples are very basic and overly simplistic, but you get the idea. The point is, I would take what most would do in one campaign and break it up into two distinctly different campaigns. Here's why:

First, each campaign should only have one purpose. This is simple to follow if each campaign has one and only one primary objective. As you build out much more elaborate and non-trivial campaigns, you'll see the necessity for this, first hand.

Second, this approach is much more scalable and logical. Isn't it logical to consider you'll likely add more lead magnets in front of this product? Maybe you'll create a lead magnet like "Three Simple Rules to Choosing an Effective Website Color Palette," which would then translate into "MK - 3 Color Rules PDF," or something similar. If you do, you'll want to keep that marketing separate from the first one. If you break out the campaigns into separate marketing and fulfillment campaigns the way I'm suggesting, it becomes trivial to do so, and very logical, as well.

I know there will be those of you who read this suggested Best Practice and ignore it. You'll argue you could still do what I'm suggesting by creating two separate logical breakdowns inside the same campaign by creating two separate paths. And you'd be correct. You could follow my advice, and create two logical campaigns inside of one physical campaign.

What I have found, though, is the campaigns are much easier to follow if you simply create them as separate physical campaigns. The reason is, when you're browsing the list of campaigns in Infusionsoft, you can easily search for the "FF"-prefixed campaigns, and find exactly what you're looking for. If you lump things together, and combine both marketing and fulfillment into a singular campaign, it becomes less obvious and more difficult to search and find later.

Remember, it is not just about what you can do, but what you should do in order for others to easily understand what you did. It is also much more clear when searching through the campaigns, because you'll see the various lead magnet-titled marketing campaigns.

4. Use Campaign Merge Fields and Links

Campaign merge fields and campaign links are two of the best features of Campaign Builder, and two of the most infrequently used, as well. Many people don't even know how to get to them, or that they even exist.

In the main campaign editing screen, look at the top right. You'll see there is a **Actions** menu with a dropdown arrow in the button. It is right to the left of the blue **Publish** button. This is a hidden gem of Campaign Builder which too many users do not even know exists. Click the button, and you will see the **Merge Fields** and **Links** options at the bottom of the menu.

You can and should use merge fields for any text you repeat throughout the campaign which you want to define once and reuse consistently. This is great for the name of your program, the date of an event, the location or directions for an event, etc. Any time there is any text you will reference multiple times in your emails. This saves you from (a) having to retype it over and over, and (b) possibly making a mistake in how you type or reference it.

Campaign links, which appear as the last menu option, are even more powerful. I use them in every single campaign I ever create, and you should, too, if you want to avoid broken links, typos and constantly editing multiple emails.

With merge links, you can define a website URL and save it as a named link at the campaign level. Then, when you are composing emails inside of your campaign in any of the sequences anywhere in the campaign, instead of typing in the URL again, you simply create the link as a campaign link, instead of a website link.

Don't underestimate the power of this simple substitution. This allows you the ability to switch quickly between testing URLs and production URLs for example. Let's say you have some URLS you're using right now just to test things and work out any bugs in your checkout process. By defining the links in the emails as campaign links, instead of hardcoding them, you can easily change them all in all of your emails in ten seconds flat, just by editing the global campaign link, instead. Super powerful.

The other obvious benefit of using campaign links is it prevents you from making typos. I don't know about you, but I've seen many emails come my way that had a typo in the link, only to be followed twenty minutes later by a "mea culpa" email, apologizing for the screw-up and sending the proper link. You can easily avoid making a simple typo by just using a campaign merge link from the beginning.

5. Save Campaign Versions (Frequently)

Using the same Campaign menu inside the Campaign Builder editing canvas, you can also access the ability to save versions of your campaigns. This does exactly what it implies. It allows you to save multiple versions of the campaign you are working on, and to restore a previous version, as well. This is a powerful feature you should be using frequently in your campaign building process to protect your work and allow you to test out variations.

IMPORTANT: *While campaign versioning is very useful, it is somewhat limited. The versions that are saved do not include the email copy. This means that if you plan to use versioning to backup a lot of email copy, you need to find a different solution. This is a disappointing limitation in my mind, but it is important you understand that versioning only saves the campaign structure, not the copy.*

You will also find the option to save a copy of your campaign in the Campaign menu. This is another power option I frequently use when I want to make a backup copy or clone of my campaign. Sometimes, for example, you need another campaign virtually identical to the one you just created, only with a few small changes. This is what I mean by a clone. I simply copy it over, and make the necessary changes, saving a ton of time by not recreating the whole campaign in the process.

6. Use Campaign Goals for Reporting (not tags)

Campaign reporting is widely misunderstood. First of all, there are two ways to report on campaigns, but most people only know of the first method.

The first Reporting method is to simply click on the Performance tab inside of the Campaign Builder. Doing so will show you where contacts are in the campaign and how many have achieved the goals within your campaign. You can also toggle the campaign to look at current contacts or historical contacts, within the past 24 hours or last 30 days. Therein lies the first misunderstanding.

Many Infusionsoft users mistakenly believe you cannot access campaign goal achievement data beyond 30 days because that's all that is shown in the performance tab data within the Campaign Builder. That's not true, and that leads us to the second reporting method.

The second Reporting method is to go outside of Campaign Builder to the **Marketing -> Reports** main menu. As you scroll through the various reports, you'll see there are several campaign reports. The most useful of these is the Campaign Goal Completion report. The data in this report is the same as if you click on the little blue man icon inside of Campaign Builder. With this report, though, you can also specify any time range you want - not just 24 hours or the past 30 days.

I know this is a very simple revelation, but the implications of this to your Best Practices approach towards Campaign Builder, as well as how you structure your campaigns, is quite profound. What I see most often is people don't understand they can report on goal completion via this report. As a result, they create tags within their campaigns as a reporting mechanism.

This is not only unnecessary; it actually slows down the performance of your Infusionsoft application. Having too many tags is the number one reason for slow apps. Worse than that, it also makes your campaigns flow poorly and not be very well documented. Instead, by using goals within your campaigns, they become much more clear and self-documenting. Remember, one of our core concepts of Infusionsoft is that it is a goal achievement system. Your campaigns should reflect that goal achievement progression and, if you do it this way, you'll be able to get any reporting data out of the system you'll ever need without having to resort to using excessive tags.

Advanced Campaign Practices

The next set of Best Practices for Campaign Builder are a bit more advanced, so I've broken them out into this separate section. They may not apply to everyone, or to your level of sophistication with Campaign

Builder at this point in your Infusionsoft experience, but I did want to provide further guidance for those who are ready for it.

7. Functional Tags & How to Avoid Them

We've talked quite a bit about functional tags - tags used to start and stop campaigns, or other functional purposes. We've talked about how they create clutter and add a lot of tag bloat to your app, as well as how excessive tag use leads to poor application performance. In short, there are a lot of reasons for not using them.

An advanced method we use is to use API Goals instead of functional tags. I'm not calling this an advanced method because it is difficult (it is actually super easy), but because it is dependent on either using the Infusionsoft API yourself, or using our MyFusion Helper app. Unfortunately, while Infusionsoft does support API goals natively in the Campaign Builder, they do not give you any way of creating them yourself. You must use an external tool or application.

You can evaluate MyFusion Helper via a free trial at this link:

http://ismastery.com/free

An API goal simply allows you to create a goal named by the application it is created with. It is designed so third party applications can create events in Infusionsoft when something happens externally.

For example, imagine you have a third party membership site, and its user management doesn't tie into Infusionsoft by default. Inside this membership software, your contacts have the option of changing their email address and this creates havoc inside of Infusionsoft. Because of this, you approach an Infusionsoft API developer and he creates a small integration that triggers an API Goal in Infusionsoft every time someone changes their email address in your membership software.

Now, you can simply drag that API Goal onto the canvas. You then add a sequence behind it that alerts you with a Task to verify the users email address, and either merge or update it accordingly. The purpose of the API Goal is to fire off an event to allow you to be able to respond to it.

Inside of MyFusion Helper, we have a Helper called the Goal It Helper. It is designed to allow you to do exactly this - create API Goals whenever you want. This way, you can use them to replace functional tags.

By using API Goals instead of functional tags, you no longer have to worry about removing those tags. You don't have to be concerned about slowing down your app from having a bunch of unnecessary tags, either. Your campaigns themselves will become much simpler, as you'll no longer require those sequences where you apply and remove the functional tags.

8. Auto-Purging Campaigns

Auto-purging campaigns are designed to allow you to use a lot of tagging during the testing phase of your campaigns, or even during the first few months of their deployment, but then have a built in mechanism for cleaning up after themselves. I use these a lot, especially in the Welcome Campaign, where I might have a lot of different tracking tags.

The process for creating auto-purging campaigns is very simple. I consider it advanced only because many people may not need it. I simply create a secondary purge campaign that has a function tag (or, as is my preference, an API Goal) that starts it. Then, it just has a single sequence with an action inside to remove a whole bunch of tags. Simply add the tags you want to remove to this action. The only trick is to put a delayed timer in front of that action to remove the tags. Then, in the main campaign, whenever a contact enters, I also apply the functional tag (or API Goal) to start them in the purge campaign, as well.

How long you want to wait before purging the tag data is really up to you. I generally find, though, six months is adequate. The way this works is pretty simple:

A contact enters your "MK - Welcome Campaign." When they do, you also start them in the "PG - Welcome Campaign." In that purge campaign, however, there is a six month delay timer preventing them from doing anything until six months from now.

The contact progresses through the "MK - Welcome Campaign." Because we're running lots of experiments and want to analyze their results, all kinds of tracking tags are being applied. 60 to 90 days later, the "MK - Welcome Campaign" terminates. All of that tagging data is still being saved, though, until we bump up against the six month delayed timer in the "PG - Welcome Campaign," since the contact is still sitting there in that campaign waiting for the timer to expire. When it does, the purge process is kicked off, the tracking tags are all removed from the contact and the "PG - Welcome Campaign" is now complete, as well.

This is simply a self-cleaning process. Think of it as allowing you to cheat on your diet today because you've already booked yourself into a weight loss clinic six months from now. Ok, maybe not the best analogy, but, hopefully, you get the point.

9. Sales Pipeline Automation

I tend to use sales pipeline automations quite a bit because, as I've previously discussed, I treat the sales pipeline as a generic workflow system. There is, however, a pretty common mistake I see many people make with their sales pipeline automations. They forget to terminate the automation with some sort of stop goal.

Let's say you have an automation when someone *moves into* a sales stage named "Create Proposal." A contact enters the stage, and an automated process is fired off to begin creating a proposal and email it out to that client. The problem is, what if the sales person accidentally put that contact in there? So, they quickly note the error they made, and move the contact into another stage.

The problem is if you don't have a termination goal inside of that "Create Proposal" campaign (which would be named "SP - Create Proposal" per my conventions), then even though you've now moved the contact into another stage, they would continue in the original automation that was started. It makes sense, because you started them in the automation, and didn't stop them. However, it is probably not the desired result.

There are two Best Practices I like to use with sales pipeline automation campaigns. First, I always like to have a delay timer as the first step of the automation. This is just a failsafe to allow for time to correct an errant mistake of putting someone into a campaign by accident. I will generally make this delay as long as possible, as long as it would not cause a problem with the normal course of action. So, if a 30-minute delay wouldn't hurt anything, that's what I'd use.

Second, I always create a *moves out of* goal at the end of the automation. To clarify, there is a goal type of "Moves an Opportunity" with the Campaign Builder. When you use this goal, there are two ways it fires. When an opportunity moves into or moves out of a stage. Typically, people will just use the *moves into* type goals. I'm suggesting you start the campaign with a *moves into* goal. Then, have your sequence(s) and, finally, terminate the campaign with a *move out of* goal.

Remember, Infusionsoft is a goal completion-based system. By terminating the campaign with a *moves out of* goal, you can stop the contact from progressing further in this campaign when they move out of the stage into another.

NOTE: This assumes you're using the default sequence setting of "Stops immediately," which is represented by the little blue flag in the bottom left corner of the sequence. If you see a green arrow in the bottom left corner of the sequence, instead, then the sequence is configured to "Runs until complete," and it will not stop when the subsequent goal is achieved. I rarely ever use this sequence type, although there are some cases for it.

10. Creating Campaigns that Can Be Paused

Restartable campaigns are not something inherently supported in Infusionsoft, but we can create them. Suppose you want to create a campaign that can be stopped and restarted later, and has the logic in it so the contact restarts right where they left off?

This can be useful for certain situations. You may have a long-term fulfillment campaign, with dozens of emails over several months. It is important people receive all of the emails, but it is also a very long campaign. You may want to periodically "pause" it so you can do a short term promotion without bombarding the contacts with too many emails. That's just one case of when you might want to use this structure.

This is an inherently complex structure, and it does take a bit of extra work to setup. My advice is to only use it if you really need it and can't find a better alternative. Furthermore, to explain this concept, I'll have to go into a lot of detail. If you don't want to use this type of logic, you might just want to skip this section.

There are a couple of alternative approaches you can use. Both require some extra work, and it just comes down to a personal preference of which route you choose to use.

The first method uses the legacy features of action sets to setup a rule that conditionally sends out an email. The second method is done entirely within Campaign Builder, but requires you to have skip logic set up to skip over emails that have been already sent. I have seen others teach both of these approaches and they both work. Unfortunately, what I have also seen taught is to use tags as the controlling logic for whether a contact has seen an email already or not (I'll discuss this in more detail in just a bit and show you a much better alternative than littering your app with thousands or even tens of thousands of unnecessary tags).

The problem with using tags is you'll need one tag for every email in the series. If it is a short series of emails, that's not such a big deal. If it is a short series of emails, though, you're not likely to use this technique to stop and restart contacts in it anyway. That means, if you're using this technique, it is likely because this is a very long sequence. That would mean tons of tags.

To illustrate, let's say there are 50 emails in this long-term nurture sequence. Let's also assume you have a list size of 20,000 contacts. That would mean, if you use a tag based solution, you'll end up creating one million tags (said with an Dr. Evil voiceover and pinky hand gesture - lol). That's just insanity!

Regardless of whether you use the legacy action set method or the purely Campaign Builder method, I recommend you track the contact's current email number via a single custom field, instead. You can accomplish the same thing, but instead of creating tens of thousands (or more) of tracking tags, you need to use just a single custom field.

The method I teach and use myself is the Campaign Builder method. I'll cover the legacy method briefly, as well, but it is not my recommendation you use it. The reason is two-fold. First, all legacy features of Infusionsoft are being depreciated and discouraged from being used going forward. Second, I just feel using the legacy action setup approach takes a lot of the logic outside of Campaign Builder and makes it much more difficult to follow. It also requires your emails be sent using legacy Templates, instead of within Campaign Builder, as well. I feel this further magnifies the risk of using depreciated features.

Regardless of which method you use, you must store the last email number the contact received, or the next email they should receive, via a whole number custom field. To do this, you use the **Set Field Value** widget in the Campaign Builder.

In the sequence, after you send out email #1, you'd also drag a **Set Field Value** widget onto the canvas. Then, set the custom field you've created to track what email they're on to the value "1". You would repeat this after every email. If you use the legacy action set approach, you'd have to set it to a value of "2" to indicate the next email they should receive (I'll explain later).

Now, independent of what method we use, we'll know where they are in their progression through the emails. Imagine a series of 50 emails, and they just received email #39. In this case, their custom field would be set to the value 39. Now, if we pulled them out of the campaign, and, later, put them back into the campaign again, we could simply skip over the first 39 emails and advance to email #40.

That's the basic logic of it. However, we still haven't talked about the two methods which contain the actual skip logic you'll need to use. Each method has pros and cons, and I've used both in different situations. Before explaining how to implement each method, I want to start by explaining the pros and cons of each.

Using the legacy action set method means you'll be creating an action set for each and every email you send out. It also means you'll have to create the emails as Templates and not use the traditional email widget in the Campaign Builder. However, the good news is the campaign itself will be fairly simplistic. You'll be able to put all of the emails (which will actually be sent via an Action Set with the send email functionality) inside a single sequence.

Using the Campaign Builder method eliminates all of the action sets. It also means the emails can be sent directly from within Campaign Builder. However, the campaign itself will be quite complex. You'll need two sequences and a decision diamond for every single email you send.

By now, you're hopefully seeing why I started this section by recommending you only resort to this type of logic if you truly need it. As you can see, either option you choose involves quite a bit of leg work to set up. If you're still reading this, you must really need this functionality... or you're just a masochist!

The legacy action set approach allows you to take advantage of the rules-based conditional logic you can apply to an action set. Many people - especially new users of Infusionsoft - are not really familiar with action sets, and very few know of the conditional rules you can set with them. If you look at a legacy action set when you apply an action, though, there is a checkbox that says, "Only run this action when certain rules are met." This is the secret sauce of action sets, and why many Infusionsoft gurus still use them.

This simple checkbox allows you to create rules that would control when an action is or isn't executed. In our case, we could create a rule that only sends out the email if the value of their custom field equals the number of the email they should receive. If you're using this method, you want to store the next email number they should receive in the custom field, rather than the last one they received. The reason is when you create the rule criteria in the legacy action set, you'll want to check if their custom field is equal to that custom field. The logic allows for equal or not equal, but doesn't allow for less than or greater than. So let's recap how this would work.

For each email, you'd have an action set widget that would execute a legacy action set for that email. The action set would use the "Send Email" action, which would send out a Template email (not from within Campaign Builder). However, the action set would be configured to only send that email if their custom field equaled the number of the next email to send them. So, if they already received email #39, the value of their custom field should be "40," and this action set rule would check to see if it equaled "40". If it didn't equal "40," it would not send out the email.

There is another issue that you'll have to address as well: The delay between emails.

As I've said, though definitely feasible, I do not recommend this approach, due to its tight coupling with legacy features that are being depreciated and slowly phased out of Infusionsoft.

The method I prefer is the Campaign Builder method. With it, you will have to create two sequences and a decision diamond for every email you send out. Yes, that really means if you're sending out 50 emails in this campaign, you'll have a giant campaign with 100 sequences.

To understand the flow of this, let's walk through the same example, and say that the contact has already received the first 39 emails. Their custom field would be set to 39. As they come to the next sequence in Infusionsoft, there would be a decision diamond that would check if their custom field value equaled "39." If it did, they'd stay on the top branch, and things would continue. If, however, their custom field did not equal "39," they'd go to the second option of the decision diamond branching logic, which would be a "blank" sequence that would simply skip them to the next sequence pair.

I want you to visualize two parallel paths or rows of sequences. On the top, you have the sequences that send out the emails. The first would send email #1. The second would send email #2, and so on. Go ahead and follow with me by opening up a blank campaign and creating this as I describe it. You only need to create three sequences though (we don't need to painfully put you through all 50).

On the second row, create a second sequence below each of the three in the top row. In the top row of three sequences, label them "Send Email #1," "Send Email #2" and "Send Email #3." On the bottom row of sequences, underneath those, label the three sequences "Skip Email #1," "Skip Email #2" and "Skip Email #3."

Now, we need to connect them to create the decision diamond logic. It is very important you connect them in the same order every time. The reason for this is when you double click on the decision diamond, it loads them in the order in which you connected them. If you connect them in different orders each time, it will flip flop back and forth with the rule logic, and that is very tough to follow. So follow this next step carefully.

First, connect the "Send Email #1" sequence to the "Send Email #2" sequence. Next, connect the "Skip Email #1" sequence to the "Send Email #2" sequence. Finally, connect the "Skip Email #1" sequence to the "Skip Email #2" sequence. Now, just repeat, paying careful attention to follow that exact same order every time. To finish off the campaign, you will need to add a start goal at the beginning and connect it to both the "Send Email #1" and the "Skip Email #1."

You'll also need to add a stop goal at the end, and connect both of the last sequences to it. For this logic to work, it is imperative all of your sequences be set to the default behavior of "Stops immediately" (which is signified by the blue flag in the bottom left). If even one of the 100 sequences you create has the "Runs till complete" setting, the entire campaign will be flawed.

Now, let's look at the logic. If they're on the top row, they will just keep progressing through the campaign, with no decision diamond branching. Let's assume you want to "pause" everyone in the campaign. Each contact would receive the stop goal (whether it is a tag or API Goal) and that would automatically and immediately pull them out of the campaign.

This is difficult for many to understand, but even when there are a 100 different sequences connected to each other, as long as they all lead to that stop goal, applying that single stop goal will immediately pull them out of the entire campaign. It doesn't matter where they are in any of the 100 sequences, as long as all of the sequences are set to their default "Stops immediately" behavior. This is super powerful.

To restart them into the campaign, you'd simply apply the start tag to the contacts, and they'd re-enter the campaign. Now this is where the fun happens, so let's walk through that logic.

Let's go back to the example of a contact that has received the first 39 emails. His custom field value is set to "39," and the contact is now re-added back into the campaign to restart and pick up where they left off. They enter the campaign, and, at each email, we check, via the decision diamond, to see if their custom field value equals 1 less than the email number. If it does, they go to the top path, send out the email and resume in the campaign. If it doesn't, they go into the lower skip path and immediately progress to the next decision diamond. Since there are no delays, or anything at all, in these blank skip sequences, they will just skip along from 1 to 2 to 3 and all the way until they hit #40.

When they get to #40, the logic will say, "if the custom field equals 39, send email 40." That will be true, and they'll go into the top row and resume where they left off. This skip logic works very well and is actually not that hard to do, once you get the hang of it. It is, however, a lot of work if you don't absolutely need it.

One important note is you will have to account for the very first time they come into this campaign, since you can get into some issues with comparing numeric values against null or empty fields with Infusionsoft. So, make sure you add some controlling logic at the very beginning of the campaign.

There is a lot of minutia in the explanation above, so I've created a video to show the process visually that you can access here:

http://ismastery.com/pause

11. Creating Template Campaigns

When you do a lot of campaign building work, you'll find you end up doing a lot of the same things over and over again. You'll quickly begin to develop your own standard campaigns, whether you realize it or not.

What I see most people do is realize the campaign they are about to create is similar to another one they did in the past. So, they spend some time figuring out which one it was, and make a copy of it. That's smart. The problem is, they then spend a bunch of time deleting stuff and cleaning it up to be re-used for their new campaign.

Now this is necessary the very first time. The cardinal sin, however, is to not save that "cleaned up" version of the previously used campaign as a "template" to be re-used again.

I always have a library of "templates" or pre-configured and semi ready-to-go campaigns at my disposal. As you create more and more, take the couple of minutes it takes to simply save "templates" along the way. The next time you need to create a similar one, you've got 60% of the work already done for you.

The only real Best Practice recommendation here is to take the time to create the templates. Another small detail I recommend is to use an obscure naming convention for template campaigns, so they're not confused with other campaigns. I use a double underscore as the prefix of my template campaigns. For example, "__ - Optional Confirmation Template".

Using templates becomes a real time saver as you progress with your Campaign Builder experience. You'll begin to develop a nice little collection of templates that make starting new campaigns that much easier, faster and consistent!

CHAPTER 10

Custom Field Best Practices

"95% of all clients I've worked with think the only custom field is a contact custom field."

One of the most powerful capabilities of Infusionsoft is the ability to define custom fields for your contacts. This allows you to customize and personalize the contact database to your own specific needs. There are, however, some limitations with custom fields. It is important to understand them so you design your systems accordingly.

Custom Field Creation Best Practices

Custom fields are created in the **Admin -> Settings -> General** section of Infusionsoft. At the very top, you'll see the Custom Fields heading and the ability to setup your custom fields. The one very simple thing many people overlook is that there are multiple types of custom fields.

Many think the only custom field is a contact custom field, or, at least, they do not use anything but contact custom fields. The reality is you can create up to 99 custom fields for each of the types of custom fields you have access to - Referral Partner custom fields, Company custom fields, Contact custom fields, Task/Appointment/Note custom fields, Order custom fields, Subscription custom fields and Opportunity custom fields.

This is a big takeaway when it comes to using custom fields within Best Practice guidelines, because the first and easiest way to not run out of custom fields is to simply make sure you're using the right type of custom field. You may, for example, be storing something on the contact record, when you could, instead, store it on the Order record. Or, maybe, you're storing pre-purchase sales-related data on the contact record when it should really be in the Opportunity record.

The second Best Practice recommendation when using custom fields is to make sure and categorize them properly by selecting (or creating) the appropriate tab and header. Infusionsoft uses tabs and headers to group and display the custom fields in the contact record detailed view. Take the time to categorize them according to how you'd like them displayed.

The good news is if you haven't done this properly (or at all) up until now, you can easily correct and implement it right away. Changing the tab or category of a custom field will not affect how it is used within the system. It will only affect how it is displayed in the detailed contact editing screen. So, feel free to clean this up now. Let's just call it your homework for this section.

The biggest limitation with custom fields is you only get 99 of them to use. At first glance, this doesn't seem like such a big deal. 99 sounds like a lot of custom fields, and it is. For most users, this will not be a big deal at all.

For the users who feel they need more than 99 custom fields, about 2% of those people have legitimate reasons for needing more and will need to find an API based custom solution.

The other 98% of them fit into one of the following two situations. The most common reason for thinking you need more than 99 fields is you've been using Infusionsoft for a long time, and have kind of willy-nilly created them without a lot of forethought. Now, you find yourself infringing upon the 99 limitation. For these situations, it just takes a little effort and a little time to go back and clean up your custom field usage. You'll likely find there are dozens of them you're not using anymore and can easily delete.

The second scenario (and some people fit into both of these scenarios) is they're using custom fields inappropriately. Don't worry. No one will call DCFS on you, but you do need to get ahold of your custom field usage and straighten it out.

The best way I've found to determine when and where to use custom fields is by asking a couple of questions. I'm going to break this section up into two situations, and the questions you should ask yourself in those situations in order to determine the best answer.

Should I use a Tag or a Custom Field?

There can definitely be confusion around whether a tag or a custom field should be used. After all, they both provide for customization and storing details related to a contact. As always, though, the devil is in the details. To best determine which is right for you, ask yourself the following questions.

What is the purpose of the custom data?

If the intent is to be able to segment out your list by a specific criteria or piece of information (either the having or not having of it), then a tag is the best answer for you. Tags allow you to easily segment out your contacts. You can quickly and simply select which contacts have what tags, and easily create multiple segments on the fly.

If you need to use the data to launch an automation campaign, then you definitely want to use a tag (or, better yet, an API Goal, as discussed in Chapter 8). This type of tag would be known as a *functional tag*, as its purpose would be to start or stop a campaign, and not to store data about a contact.

If you need to store specific data relevant to only that one contact, such as their contract renewal date, you would definitely want to use a custom field. Custom fields are intended to store contact specific data. Make sure, however, you select the right field type depending upon how you wish to use that data in the future. There are multiple types of text, numeric and date fields, and they all have their pros and cons. Make sure you're selecting the right type of field. I'll go into more detail on that a little later on in the chapter.

If you're planning on merging the data into your emails in the future, you need a custom field, because tags cannot be merged into emails. Tags, however, can be used for conditional logic in decision diamonds to determine which path a contact is sent down in a campaign. Do you need to store multiple values for the same contact? If this is the case, it gets a little bit fuzzy. You may choose to use tags, and associate more than one tag with the contact. You could also, however, create a list box custom field type. List boxes do allow you to select multiple options, but they are pretty limiting when it comes to how you look at that data and search against it. So, choose carefully here.

Before you decide to use a custom field...

You only have 99 custom fields for each type, so make sure you really need it first.

After you've decided it is truly necessary, ask yourself if there is another record type to store this custom field data that would work equally well (or better) than storing it on the contact record. Remember, you also have custom fields available on the Referral Partner, Company, Task/Appointment/Note, Order, Subscription and Opportunity records as well. If you can use one of those instead of the Contact record, you definitely should, as it will save your Contact record custom fields for other situations that can't fit elsewhere.

Next, consider using a different data storage option instead of a custom field. For example, is the data something that makes better since to be stored in a Contact Note, instead of a custom field? Or, maybe you can accomplish what you need with a tag? Or perhaps the data is perfectly fine just being appended to the Person Notes field?

Another good practice for reducing your custom field usage, is to use the *Append to Contact Notes* option in a Web Form (mentioned above), instead of actually creating a new custom field. This is not a good option if you're going to need to use the custom field data in a merged email, but, in many cases where you just need to add some notes to the contact, it is adequate.

There is one other creative solution I rarely see clients and Infusionsoft users take advantage of. It is definitely a Best Practice recommendation, not only because it reduces custom field usage, but also because it is more specific and customized to your particular use of Infusionsoft. The solution I am talking about is the ability to customize the field labels for the default fields inside of Infusionsoft. To access these system labels, go to the **Admin -> Settings -> Application** menu, and look at the top under the System Labels heading.

Let's say, for example, you have no intention of ever using the Contact.AssistantName, Contact.AssistantPhone, Contact.Birthdate, Contact Address 3 fields (several), Contact Fax fields (does anyone even use a fax machine these days?), Contact.MiddleName or Contact.Nickname fields - or any of the other infrequently used fields, like Contact.SpouseName. Think through this carefully before you change them, but if you are never going to use some of those fields, you can simply rename their label, which determines how they are shown in the Infusionsoft interface.

You could, for example, rename the Contact.Birthdate field to "Contract Renewal Date," if you needed a custom date field and had no intention of ever tracking contacts birthdates. This is a very creative and efficient solution which can easily free up a dozen or more custom fields for you.

What type of custom field data type should I use?

This is another big question you should take the time to answer before just willy-nilly creating a custom field, and then later determining it won't work properly for you. I have seen this happen time and time again. A client will create, for example, a custom field to store a date/time value, and choose the Date/Time field type - seems logical.

Later, when they're working in Campaign Builder, they'll realize there isn't a way to use a Date/Time field type in Field Timers, which only support the Date data type. Little things like this can be troublesome, so take the time to investigate which field type makes sense. In general, I rarely ever use the Date/Time field for this very reason.

There are several different numeric field types, as well, so make sure you're using the one you need. I tend to only use currency, yes/no, or whole number fields, but you might have a specific reason for using a decimal field.

Likewise, when it comes to textual data, there are several options. One of the big mistakes I see is the use of a Text data type, when what is really desired is a Text Area for large amounts of free form text. Another issue I often see is people storing web site addresses and URLS in Text fields. That is fine, but if you use a Website field instead, Infusionsoft will make that a clickable address via a little blue arrow at the right-hand side of the input box. That can be a nice time saver.

Also relating to textual data, you can use Dropdowns instead of a Text field. This is a great option if you want to limit what a person stores in the field, but still give them choices. This will keep your data much cleaner. The Dropdown data type is also better for decision diamond-type logic because you can easily select the values, as opposed to typing them in and making a typo.

Only One Specific Use

A common, and very confusing, issue I see when auditing clients campaigns is that they reuse custom fields for multiple purposes in multiple campaigns. This is a very poor practice. Not only is it confusing, but it can also lead to data contamination as well as logic failures in your campaigns.

Only use a custom field for one specific purpose. If, later, it becomes a multi-use field by multiple campaigns, rename the custom field and thoroughly document its "shared" usage. You can rename a custom field without impacting your existing campaigns.

What you will see is that the name you are using is really only a label. The internal field name used by Infusionsoft internally and through the API does not actually change. You can see this for yourself by clicking on the **View the field database names (for the API)** link in the **Admin -> Settings -> General -> Set up custom field names** section of the app. Clicking that link will show your name for the custom field as well as the internal API name.

Other Considerations

One last special case for you to consider is how Infusionsoft uses NULL values. The NULL is a special case, and you need to always take it into account in your campaign logic.

For example, let's say you have a field that is a Whole Number. When you create a new contact, that contact does not have a value in this custom field. It is not a 0, either. It is simply NULL - or not populated. You have to be careful how your decision diamond branching logic handles this NULL case and test things out. NULL values can surprise you and lead to erratic campaign behavior.

Do not get confused by how the value appears in the Infusionsoft interface either. If you open up a contact with that custom whole number field mentioned above, it will show a 0, even though there might be a NULL in the field.

There are lots of other field type choices, but remember, the purpose of this book is not to exhaustively cover every single iota of detail, which can easily be sought out online via Infusionsoft's Help resources. The purpose of this book is to give you the 20% of the Best Practices you can apply to save yourself time by avoiding the big mistakes many make from not knowing about the best way to do things.

CHAPTER 11

Order Processing Best Practices

"No numbers can ever be trusted as repeatable in your niche, but can just serve to illustrate the next experiment you should consider running."

The most critical part of the marketing process is actually processing the sale. Unfortunately, it is often neglected or only given casual attention. I want to be very clear on this point. The single fastest way to scale up your business is to optimize the purchase process. To illustrate this, I want to give you a case study.

Frank runs a high volume information marketing business, and leverages his NY Times Best Selling author status to really drive a ton of leads into his system. His system has evolved over the years, but in many ways, has stayed pretty much the same.

The sales process was working, and working well. Most would be very happy with the numbers he was achieving. When I looked at the process and, especially, the volume of people going through the system, though, I knew we had lots of opportunity to radically improve and refine the system. Frank was adding between 200 and 250 leads per day through his funnel. Most of them were from Adwords, so they were highly targeted and responsive leads.

Frank normally does launches that result in six-figure sales in just 4 or 5 days. When we approached the first funnel, I was less than excited to see it was his worst-selling product. I asked him what he expected to sell on the launch, and he said, "$9,000." Really? Again, I was quite disappointed. He said, "Yeah. This is a re-launch, and it didn't sell well the first time. It only sold, $18,000, and I have never sold more than 50% of my initial sales volume on a re-launch. On top of that, I'm only going to be sending it to small segment of my list." So there it was. The bar (a very low one) had been set.

To make matters worse, we only had a few days (three) to get this all in place, so we wouldn't really have time to make serious changes. Because of the time constraints, we didn't change the copy in the emails, or on the sales pages, and we didn't have time to split test price points or upsells. However, when our launch got rolling, Frank was blown away by the results.

On Day 1, we almost broke $20,000 in sales. Now again, this is not a big number, but remember, his entire first launch of this product only did $18,000 in sales. So, in Day 1, we had already more than exceeded his original launch, and more than 2x'ed his expectations. At the end of the re-launch, we did a whopping $47,484 in sales - more than 500% of the $9,000 he had expected!

If we didn't change the copy, and we didn't change the offer, and we didn't change the price, and we didn't change the upsells, just what DID we change?

Well, given the extremely short three-day timeline, we focused on making the entire process more efficient, streamlined and congruent. We didn't change the copy on the sales pages, but we redid their design with new landing page software that generates very clean and elegant landing pages (we used Thrive Themes, if you are interested). On the landing pages, we emphasized trust in the checkout process by enhancing the seals near the Buy button.

The biggest change, however, was on the checkout form itself. We completely overhauled the order form, making it mobile-friendly, clean and elegant. We also added social proof and testimonials to the order form itself and, again, emphasized the trust seals and congruency with the main offer. The order form was night and day different (and better) than the original.

Lastly, we overhauled the 1-click upsell pages, as well, also using the Thrive Themes landing page builder for them. We didn't change any of the copy. We just optimized and cleaned up the design: bigger buttons, clean and clear design, cleaned up the video hosting and presentation, de-emphasized the "no thanks" option and other tweaks.

It is an odd thing do say, but if you look at what we did with Frank's funnel, we didn't fundamentally change anything... but we refined everything! All of those small refinements boosted his sales 260% over his original launch, and 527% over his expectations for this re-launch. Are these typical results? Of course not, and to make sure I'm getting in my FTC disclaimer, I make no promises or warrantees that you will ever reach these types of results.

However, this case study does illustrate just how powerful the checkout process is in your overall revenue potential and profitability. Here's the funny thing: there are at least a dozen things we should have done - all of which would have improved the results - that we didn't have time to do in this first pass. Imagine if we had the time to split test the copy, the emails, the price points, the order form, the upsells and downsells. We didn't even add the easiest thing we could have - an abandoned cart sequence. There's absolutely no way we wouldn't have added at least another 30% in sales if we had been able to do all of that.

Now that I've set the stage and shown you this stuff really does work, let's jump into the rest of the Chapter and talk about the various elements of a Best Practices approach to your order forms and checkout process.

Mobile Friendly Order Forms - A Must

Today, more than 60% of web searches are executed on a mobile phone or tablet device. Desktop, and even notebook computers, are quickly going the way of the gas-guzzling muscle cars of the 70's. Yeah, some people still want their performance, but the vast majority are opting for convenience, instead.

What I find even more disruptive in this trend, is not the simple shift from desktop to mobile or tablet, but the more intrinsic shift from generic browsing and searching to highly-optimized mobile apps. In other words, people are not just using Google like they used to. Today, "There's an app for that!" is the common response to most any question. What that means is, mobile is not just a trend. It is a disruptive shift in the way people do business online.

There are a lot of buzzwords in the marketing and business sectors, so be careful you're not buying into the hype. There's a big difference between mobile-*responsive* and mobile-*optimized*. Many tools, platforms and shopping carts call themselves "mobile-friendly" or "mobile-responsive." That hardly means they are mobile-*optimized*. Many have done just some basic level changes to make them "better" on mobile devices, but that hardly means they are "good," much less "excellent," on a mobile platform.

Mobile-optimized is what you should be shooting for. I'm not just talking about a buzzword, I'm talking about the actual experience. If you're not grabbing your handy iPhone and testing the checkout process through your own funnel, I can guarantee you, you are losing money. And likely, a ton of it.

Yes, I did say iPhone and no, that was not a simple bias (though I readily admit I am, indeed, biased toward Apple devices). Here is a fact: the demographics of an iPhone user, versus the demographics of an Android user, are very, very different. iPhone users have much higher average gross and disposable income levels than Android users.

If you look at the details of your sales made from mobile phones, it is quite probable the iPhone sales will be 2x to 4x the sales of those on Android devices. Obviously, you need to test those numbers yourself in your niche, because if there's one thing this book should have taught you by now, everything varies by niche and your particular market demographic. No numbers can ever be trusted as repeatable in your niche, but can just serve to illustrate the next experiment you should run.

In the next few months, I predict you'll see wildly adaptive checkout processes based upon the device you're on. I don't just mean things such as how the page looks or is formatted, but actual different check out processes. For example, Stripe.com has become wildly successful in the industry with very minimalist checkout forms for mobile, where all you need is your name, email, credit card number and a zip code.

In the near future, highly successful carts will customize the entire checkout form so users on a desktop might still be asked for their billing information, but users on a mobile device would go without it. Also, look for options like Apple Pay and Android Pay to have a big impact on this, as well. Carts will begin to integrate at such an intrinsic level with mobile devices, to complete a mobile purchase, all people will have to do is simply scan their thumbprint.

If you are not investing heavily into highly optimizing your checkout process for mobile right now, you are throwing away serious piles of money in your business. I simply cannot state it any more directly than that. The case study above really illustrates that, as well. The biggest changes we made in Frank's funnel were all about making it more mobile optimized.

The Worst Number in Business - "1"

I couldn't possibly write a chapter on order and payment processing without the topic of merchant account diversification. Anyone who has been around this industry for many years, as I have, or has done more than a million online, can tell you at least a couple of "war stories" regarding merchant processors. The really funny part is I've heard the same stories time and time again, and they really are not at all specific to the processor. In other words, no matter what merchant processor you use, you are just as likely to have a problem at some point. It is a simple law of averages.

I have personally had PayPal temporarily seize tens of thousands of dollars, for no reason. This did not just happen once, but twice! They froze the account while they "investigated" some theory of theirs, and then eventually returned all of the funds and apologized - twice. It did not matter that I had a nearly perfect and unblemished record with them. It did not matter I was not in the info-product or make money online space, and was actually selling services to small businesses. The point is, I would have been in serious trouble if I did not have multiple merchant accounts, and if you do not heed this advice, someday, you will be as well.

That's why I say the worst number in business is the number "one." If you have one of anything, you are in serious risk. One merchant provider? Big no-no. Only have one hosting company? Not a good idea. You get the point.

In Infusionsoft, you can setup multiple merchant accounts, and I highly recommend you have at least two. Recently, Infusionsoft introduced their own merchant integration called Infusionsoft Payments. It takes only five minutes to setup and gain approval. This is an integration with WePay and provides Stripe-like pricing and simplicity. My recommendation is, if you're not already using it, you at least sign up and run a little bit of money through it as a backup merchant. This way, at least, you'll have multiple accounts you could use, if necessary.

In the past, Infusionsoft let you rotate your checkouts through multiple merchants. That feature is no longer available. However, you can still use multiple merchants very easily. At the order form level in Infusionsoft, you can set or override the merchant account to be used.

As a Best Practice, what I recommend, doing prior to any big launch, is to have your order forms cloned. Each with a different merchant provider. Then, on your checkout pages, instead of linking directly to the actual order form, link to a redirect.

If you route your clicks through Pretty Link first, you can easily change where they go later, without having to make any alterations to code, checkout pages, order forms or anything else. So, in the middle of your launch, if you start having problems with merchant A, you simply change the redirect to send your purchases to merchant B. More powerfully, you can even use split testing to send them to multiple processors from the beginning, sending 50% of the sales to merchant A, and 50% to merchant B.

When working with large 7 and 8-figure level marketers, this is the type of configuration I always put in place. Sometimes, they even have 3 or 4 merchants when doing a large launch, to mitigate risk even further. The truth is this process is so simple and can be done with the free version of Pretty Link (or other redirect scripts), everyone should do it. It only takes an extra minute to make a copy of your order form and change the merchant. It only takes another minute to create a simple redirect. Anyone can have this safety net in place and ready to go without skipping a beat for the grand total of $0 and two minutes of invested time.

Should You Use Infusionsoft Order Forms?

Given all of the emphasis I've put on the order checkout process and the importance of mobile optimized checkout, you might be surprised by my answer. The truth is, it depends on your situation. For the vast majority of my clients, they aren't doing the kind of volume of sales Frank is, or have a list of over 250,000 subscribers.

If you do a low volume of sales transactions (I'm not talking about dollar amounts, but, rather, the number of transactions), and, especially, if you're selling high-end services, you really don't need to worry about this, and should be just fine using the Infusionsoft order forms. High-ticket sales customers are buying for reasons much deeper than a simple order form inconvenience will sway.

However, if you're running paid traffic to low-ticket, impulse buy, informational and digital offers, you need to remove every possible barrier to purchase. In this case, I really don't recommend a native Infusionsoft order form, as it is simply not a mobile optimized form. Recently they have switched them to be mobile aware, and they are better, but are still a far cry from mobile optimized.

A Purchase Is a Purchase Is a Purchase - Not!

One of the ugly warts of Infusionsoft (yes, it has some warts, and I told you I'd be candid about them) is there are various ways of triggering a payment. In fact, there are three methods. The problem with this is, these three methods don't all behave the same. Depending on your particular needs, you'll need to really make sure the system is configured to serve you.

Purchase Goals in the Campaign Builder are not the same as E-Commerce Purchase Actions, and neither of those are the same as Billing Automation Purchase Triggers. All of these fire off in different situations.

I want you to realize these three do not behave the same, and that you really must investigate this according to your system usage. For example, Campaign Builder purchase goals don't fire if the original purchase fails due to a credit card decline, even if the person subsequently updates their credit card successfully. That means, if you don't take specific actions, they won't ever get into their fulfillment campaigns, and actually get the product they paid for. This means chargebacks, payment disputes and unhappy clients for you.

The best advice I can give you is to consult the link below. It will take you to the specific, most current help document from Infusionsoft. It illustrates the different behaviors between these three styles of purchase goals. Beyond that, test and verify. I am making the link go through my own redirect so I can easily update it in the future if Infusionsoft changes the page with one of their updates, and also to save you typing in a big long URL into the browser.

http://ismastery.com/actions

Keep in mind Infusionsoft releases monthly updates to the product, which include bug fixes, enhancements and new features. It is entirely possible the couple of situations I raised above may be resolved when you read this book. That is why I'm telling you to please check the link above for the most updated information.

The bottom line is there are three different methods for invoking purchase goals, and they don't necessarily work the same, or as expected. Spend some time verifying their operation in your particular business and/or configuration.

Credit Card Declines & Expiring Credit Cards

I hope you know Infusionsoft does have automation hooks for both expiring credit cards, as well as payment failures. I say this because, in analyzing hundreds of Infusionsoft businesses over the years, I've found that only about 35% to 40% of businesses are using the built-in tools effectively, much less going beyond the basic options.

Just to be clear, Infusionsoft does allow you, via Billing Automation, to set up triggers to email your contacts when their credit card is about to expire. They also have triggers that fire off when a credit card fails, and you have the ability to capture those events and respond to the contact via email, as well.

Another little known fact is Infusionsoft also has built-in global actions that fire off when a contact clicks on a credit card update link, or actually updates their credit card. Of the 35% to 40% of clients I've seen who historically have billing automation and credit card expiration triggers, fewer than 10% of them actually use the global actions.

These global actions allow you to know if your efforts to get the contact to update their card actually worked or not. This is why using them is vital. The Best Practice recommendation here is to always set a goal (I use an API Goal via MyFusion Helper, but you could also use a tag goal if you like) when the credit card is updated. This way, your campaign sequence can terminate, and you can also track the effectiveness of your dunning process.

For a free trial of MyFusion Helper you can go to this link:

http://ismastery.com/free

Remember my mantra: every campaign is, first and foremost, an experiment. Your dunning campaigns are no different. You need to be tracking the effectiveness of your dunning campaigns, and monitoring if they are working or not. If they're not, and if the volume of transactions you're doing warrants it, consider using a third-party dunning solution. There are many available these days. A good quality dunning service will only charge based on the money they recover for you.

You should also note there is an inherent flaw in the logic employed by Infusionsoft regarding expiring credit cards. Yes, Infusionsoft does allow you to email contacts before their credit card expires, and it does allow you to check if they've updated their credit card via the global action in **E-Commerce -> Settings -> Orders** area. You have all of the tools you need to handle this. To date, though, I have never seen a single client proactively implement logic to protect them from this flaw properly.

The flaw is if the contact does not update their credit card, and it is indeed expired, and if that contact has a payment plan or subscription, not only will they never be charged, but you'll never be notified, either. The reason is Infusionsoft is smart enough to know there is no reason to attempt billing on an expired card, so it doesn't even try. Since it doesn't try to bill them, it won't fire off the billing failure notifications, and you'll be left in the dark that a client is simply not paying you. This is why I've listed this in Chapter 11 as one of the campaigns every Infusionsoft app should have.

One last tactic I use often with billing failures and credit card expirations is what I call the $0 Order Form. Basically, by applying some custom styling code to a standard Infusionsoft order form, and setting up a $0 product, you can create a credit card update form that doesn't charge the contact anything, but does allow them to securely enter their credit card information into an order form. Essentially, as far as Infusionsoft is concerned, they are making a $0 purchase.

What's nice about this approach is, since it is a purchase, you can setup a simple purchase goal, and automate around it. If you'd like to see an example of what this type of form would look like, you can go here:

http://ismastery.com/update

I find this is a more elegant form for people to use than the default links Infusionsoft includes in their credit card update links. There is, however, one serious limitation to using this form. The problem is it just adds or updates a credit card to the clients generic contact record.

It does not, update their actual subscription or payment plan to use the newly updated card. To solve that, you'll have to do it manually. I recommend you use the purchase goal automation with a sequence that assigns a task to yourself, or one of your staff, to update their payment plan and/or subscription to reflect the newly added or updated credit card.

A Word About the Infusionsoft Shopping Cart

So, here comes another one of those ugly wart conversations. The fact is the Infusionsoft shopping cart is very dated, and not recommended for most situations. It is fine for about 30% to 40% of the Infusionsoft user base who just need some very basic shopping cart functionality, but it breaks down very quickly with shipping and other limitations.

First off, there are two methods for using the Infusionsoft shopping cart. The first is to use their actual hosted storefronts. I can honestly and sincerely say, in several years of using and supporting Infusionsoft, and working with hundreds of clients in that timeframe, there has never been a single time when I have recommended the Infusionsoft storefront. I think that pretty much sums up my advice on the topic.

The second option, however, is using the Infusionsoft shopping cart with your own site and design. While this still has all of the limitations of shipping issues, and just generally being quite out of date, it is still viable. I have several clients using it who have small volume and small numbers of products, as well as pretty simplistic shipping needs. So, it is possible to use it effectively.

That being said, for the majority of serious E-Commerce-style sites, I recommend one of two options to my clients as a Best Practice for Infusionsoft integration, ease of use, simplicity and elegance. Either a WooCommerce + InfusedWoo platform, or a Shopify + Revenue Conduit combination. Please note, in either situation, there will be the requirement for external plugins, which come with their own sets of monthly fees. You will have to evaluate which path makes the most sense for you.

Small to medium storefronts that are fairly simplistic can easily be done within Shopify. You can then use Revenue Conduit to get that information into Infusionsoft in real time. Shopify has a beautiful interface, an exhaustive source of themes, and is widely recognized as the best in the industry for hosted E-Commerce solutions. Revenue Conduit, likewise, is widely recognized as the best way to integrate Shopify (and other supported platforms) with Infusionsoft, and I have several clients using their solution. It is elegant, and includes several campaigns they setup for you in your Infusionsoft account to help you get even more sales through your E-Commerce funnel.

Larger platforms, or platforms that require extensive customization, however, should look at using WooCommerce and InfusedWoo as a solution instead. There is definitely much more work in going this route, but it is also much more customizable to your exact specifications. WooCommerce is merely a Wordpress plugin, and InfusedWoo sits in-between WooCommerce and Infusionsoft. This platform is very solid, and

I personally use it in one of my businesses. As I said, though, it does require more customization than Shopify + Revenue Conduit.

Many people really attack Infusionsoft hard for its weak E-Commerce built-in platform and features, and rightfully so. However, my take on this is very different. I honestly could care less about using Infusionsoft as an E-Commerce platform, or even about its order forms and checkout processes. I also don't care about its lackluster design support for landing pages and web forms. In fact, if I were CEO for a day, I would actually remove all of those features from Infusionsoft, because I don't really use or recommend any of them.

To me, Infusionsoft is a very powerful and rich CRM with the best-in-class marketing automation platform available today, along with an extensible API. Those are the core features of Infusionsoft that make it well worth the cost, regardless of the other limitations. I don't worry about its weaknesses. Instead, I play to its strengths, and that's what I recommend you do as a Best Practices approach to getting the most out of Infusionsoft as possible.

Use the best-of-breed options in the marketplace to supplement and integrate with Infusionsoft, and focus your efforts with Infusionsoft on the marketing automation, CRM and data integration aspects, instead. Having said that, it is vital anything you plug into Infusionsoft views Infusionsoft's CRM as the master of all data, and that all transactional and purchase data get back into Infusionsoft. If you don't do that, you are crippling its automation capabilities, and it will have a big impact on your bottom line.

The complaints I hear over and over again are, if you follow my advice, you'll need several other plugins and integrations, and all of those drive up the true cost of ownership of Infusionsoft. Yes and yes. And, ya know what? That's a good thing. Because you shouldn't be implementing any of them without ROI, and if the ROI is there, you shouldn't care about the investment. The beauty of it is you have a platform that has those tools and integrations available to it. Rather than looking at it as a limitation, I see it as a big benefit in the marketplace. So, use best of breed solutions and plugins to enhance Infusionsoft, and don't think of it as a limitation. The real power is in the data and the automation.

1-Click Upsells and Smart Upsells

I couldn't write a chapter on Best Practices for orders and purchasing without discussing 1-Click upsells and smart upsells. I've discussed 1-Click upsells a bit in the book already, so you should be familiar with them. A true 1-click upsell comes after an initial purchase, and does not require the user to enter any information to make the purchase. It merely asks them to click a button to add the offer to their order.

This process is so simple and so effective, I don't recommend you ever put out a promotion or sale of anything without having at least one 1-Click upsell attached to it. In more costly paid traffic campaigns, having a second upsell generally makes even more sense. I do not, however, go beyond two upsells, as there is a point of diminishing returns regarding the revenue they generate and the customer satisfaction (or lack thereof) in the overall purchase process.

1-Click upsells are especially powerful when you direct all of your offers through the same upsell funnel into your core product or service. This allows you to get a lot of data quickly, analyze it, improve it and add more sales of your core offering within a short period of time.

The concept of smart upsells leverages Infusionsoft's automation and rich CRM capabilities to give even higher yield and personalization. Using a third party solution such as MyFusion Helper – free trial available at http://ismastery.com/free – you can make your Thank You pages dynamic according to the contact's individual purchase history, tags, or other criteria.

Let's say, for example, you are upselling a product. If you knew your contact had already bought that product, wouldn't it make much more sense to offer them a different upsell, instead? Don't you think that could impact your bottom line? Of course it will, and that's exactly what a smart upsell feature does.

Instead of sending the person blindly down one path, it looks at their tags, custom fields or purchase history, and then conditionally sends them to different paths. Personalized, custom and timely messaging and offers - that is what successful automation is really about. Now, again, some will complain you can't do this inside of Infusionsoft automatically. I choose to be thankful Infusionsoft is so well recognized in the industry, that many other 7 and 8-figure businesses have been built on the backs of just supporting and enhancing it.

Cart Abandonment

Last, but certainly not least in this chapter of order processing and checkout Best Practices, is a discussion of cart abandonment. I have seen estimates that claim as many as 68% of shopping cart purchases are abandoned. I'm not entirely sure I believe that high of a number, but I can tell you it will vary dramatically across niches (like everything else), and that it will certainly be above 40% to 50%. So, even if you take my more conservative numbers, you are still looking at losing one out of every two sales to cart abandonment.

I left this topic for last in the chapter because it is so powerful, and has the quickest potential to dramatically improve your revenue (if you have a decent volume of monthly transactions). There are various methods for combating cart abandonment. Some you can do inside of Infusionsoft, some you can do with plugins and enhancements to Infusionsoft, and others require a complete 3rd party solution.

The easiest cart abandonment strategy is to simply track the link clicks that lead to an order form by applying an *Abandoned Cart* tag to them. Then, when someone purchases, you remove that tag. You use automation 20 or 30 minutes after the original link click to check for the presence of the *Abandoned Cart* tag. If it is still there, that means they didn't complete the purchase, and you can launch them into a cart abandonment and objection handling sequence to try harder to get the sale.

This is so simple, anyone can do it with the built-in tools within Infusionsoft. You should be doing it on every single product sale. Remember, if you are conservatively losing one out of every two sales without it, adding it in could add a nice chunk of change into your bank account.

The past Black Friday, I ran a promotion for a client. They were not very savvy with their marketing, and I didn't want to overwhelm them with a discussion of cart abandonment. We also had a short deadline. So, rather than educating them on it, I simply did it for them instead.

I added the very basic cart abandonment strategy discussed above. I set up tracking for it, and I kept it really simple. This was just a last minute addition I personally did to go above and beyond for the client. I took the 80/20 approach and added two simple emails into the cart abandonment series. Just two emails. One emailed to them 27 minutes after they left the cart, and the second emailed to them the next day.

With just those two emails, we improved his sales by an incredible 47% on that Black Friday promotion. That is a very high number, and not at all normal. More realistic and typical numbers I generally see are in the 18% to 25% range. In this case, however, I think it was particularly effective because of the fact it was a Black Friday promotion, and people were already stirred up into a buying frenzy. On top of that, the offer was super compelling as well.

The point, however, is not whether it did 47% or 18%. The point is if you are not implementing some form of cart abandonment sequences in your marketing, you're losing money, and, likely, a lot of money.

Another way to make this even more robust is to use more optimized, third-party solutions, specifically designed to be best-of-breed solutions for just this one problem. They can get quite sophisticated, so you'll just have to shop around to see what makes sense for you. Remember the cardinal rule, though. If they can't integrate their data back into Infusionsoft, then don't use them.

Following these Best Practices will allow you to generate more sales, and increase the overall efficiency of your marketing process.

CHAPTER 12

Essential Campaigns Every App Should Have

"It is important you shift away from simple marketing campaigns, and begin to think at a much higher level of efficiency."

One of the things highly effective Infusionsoft marketers do, is set up a lot of campaigns that run on autopilot. These campaigns are designed to bring people back to their products and services, or to automate some core system functionality.

To provide the best value possible in this Best Practices guide, I felt it was critical to include a chapter on some Best Practices campaigns I feel every business should have, regardless of their niche, specialty or business type. Don't confuse these campaigns with traditional marketing campaigns for products and services. These are system level campaigns that are applicable to any business.

It is important you shift away from simple marketing campaigns, and begin to think at a much higher level of efficiency. One of the most important concepts I introduced in Chapter 2 was the concept of *Responsive Engagement*.

Responsive Engagement is all about using automation to create scenarios where contacts cross over certain thresholds, or trigger certain conditions, that automatically launch them into a marketing or re-engagement campaign. Fundamentally, however, Responsive Engagement marketing is all about looking for opportunities to send the right message, to the right person, at the right time.

In this chapter, I'm going to give you some details on campaigns that will either fit into the Responsive Engagement style of campaign, or are simply fundamental system campaigns. Either way, they will apply to every business, regardless of niche or business type. Keep in mind, however, my intent is not to give you a step-by-step campaign creation tutorial in this book. To do so would turn this book into a 1500- page dissertation, and would bore you stiff. Rather, I'm going to give you the 30,000-foot view of the campaign. Furthermore, that other level of campaign training is far more effective via video. If you want additional resources for these campaigns, I have compiled my own personal list of the tools I use. You can review it here:

http://ismastery.com/tools

This book is all about the best way to do things. Sometimes, that means going outside of the core functionality of Infusionsoft. So, some of these campaigns in both categories may require additional tools or API level interactions in order to implement them. Where required or suggested, they will be noted.

I use the word campaign in this chapter - and throughout the book – as an expression of a logical concept. I do not necessarily mean, when you save it in Infusionsoft, it should only be represented as one physical campaign in the campaign list. Sometimes, a logical campaign I implement may be comprised of several different physical campaigns that are inter-linked. The group of them forms one logical campaign.

Fundamental System Campaigns

I have developed these campaigns over the past several years to fill in missing gaps of functionality in Infusionsoft, and to automate aspects of Infusionsoft I believe should be done on every single installation. No system is perfect, and there are certain things the core system just doesn't do that I feel it should.

1. The Welcome Campaign

I devoted an entire chapter (Chapter 6) to how to craft an ideal Welcome Campaign. There is no need to go into this again in extensive detail. It is not really a campaign missing from Infusionsoft, because it must be completely custom tailored by you.

The reason this campaign is included here is simply to remind you of the structure and concept of having a Welcome Campaign that every new contact goes through. This is more of a mindset than anything else, but because I see it implemented so poorly in the industry, I felt it important to remind you of it here once again. Also, do not forget the many feeder campaigns you will create for your lead magnets, that feed into your Welcome Campaign.

2. The Email Hygiene Campaign

Just like good dental hygiene is necessary to keep your teeth healthy (and just to keep your teeth at all), the same is true for your email marketing system. Good email hygiene is not only necessary to keep your marketing firing on all cylinders, but also just to keep your account active. If you ignore good email hygiene practices, you'll likely end up getting in trouble with Infusionsoft's email compliance department, and put your app at risk.

Infusionsoft gives you some tools to help with email hygiene. The first one is the email status automation triggers. The second is the global email opt out action. They really leave it up to you, however, to properly set up and implement these tools. Be sure to do so.

You need to set up your email hygiene campaign to manage your bounced emails, as well as your opt outs. The one piece Infusion leaves out, but I feel is critical in this process, is the fact there is a big difference between how you want to do this for customers and for contacts who have never purchased anything from you.

Non-customer contacts can simply be purged from your app. Customers, on the other hand, should be kept, because of the previous purchase history you don't want to lose. What I do for our clients is automate this with our MyFusion Helper app. It can look at purchase history using the Customer Lifetime Value Helper, so we can make that determination in real time from within an automation campaign.

A second critical step is to export a backup copy of contacts you are purging, as well as to add them into a Facebook Custom Audience. Just because they are no longer on your email list does not mean you can't still market to them via Facebook. So, do not lose this opportunity. Exporting to a CSV can be done via a fulfillment report hack. The Facebook Realtime Custom Audience synchronization can be automated with MyFusion Helper as well – available for free trial at http://ismastery.com/free.

3. Handling Credit Card Expirations

Infusionsoft does support automation triggers to email people when their credit card is about to expire, but, as I mentioned in Chapter 11, it has one very serious flaw. If the contact has an active payment plan or recurring billing subscription, and they fail to update their credit card and it expires, the system will never try to bill that card.

At first, this seems logical, and it is. Why would you want Infusionsoft to try and bill an invalid credit card? You wouldn't, but since it doesn't even try, you'll never get a billing automation failure. Thus, you'll never have a warning that the billing failed.

Imagine this scenario. The contact's credit card is about to expire, and they ignore the two or three warning emails you send them to update their credit card through the credit card expiration triggers. As a result, their third payment for $197 on a 3-pay payment plan comes due... and nothing happens. The system doesn't try to process the payment because it knows the credit card is invalid, and neither you nor the client is alerted to the payment failure, either. That's a big problem, and I see this affect lots of clients.

You need to create a campaign that accounts for this "hole" in the system, and do some clever automation to try and automate the scenario, or manually resolve the situation. You could automatically create a help desk ticket, for example, or you could, at least, create a task that is assigned to someone who will manually double check the payment plan and/or reach out to the client personally.

The biggest issue is most of the client apps I have examined over the years have the billing failure notifications set up at some level, but very few use the expiring credit card notifications. The only way you can plug this hole, or fix this flaw, is if you are using both. The billing failure triggers will simply never be triggered if their credit card expires.

4. Engagement Tracking

There are many ways and methods to track engagement within Infusionsoft. The important part is not so much the method you choose, but the fact you take the time to put a system in place.

People tend to get very possessive about their lists, and hate to purge inactive contacts. The truth is, though, you are hurting your email deliverability by having dead contacts on your list. These dead contacts may also trigger spam traps, or honey pots.

ISPs (email service providers) recycle old emails that used to be valid, but have become inactive when a user leaves their service. They then take ownership of that email account themselves, and monitor if you continue emailing to it, even if that person never engages with you. In other words, they are watching you. More important, they're testing you and your email practices.

If you have a solid email engagement tracking system in place, you'll automatically purge inactive emails over time. If you don't, though, you'll likely trigger these spam traps. That can damage your email reputation, and even cause you trouble with Infusionsoft Terms of Service and email compliance, as well.

The ideal implementation would track how long it has been since your contact has opened an email or clicked on a link. It would then attempt to re-engage them automatically at set intervals of non-engagement. For example, after 60-days of not opening an email or clicking on a link, you would automatically add them into a re-engagement sequence. This sequence of emails would be designed specifically to get them to open and click, thus bringing them back into the fold of an active subscriber.

This campaign would also integrate with the Email Hygiene campaign to purge inactive contacts with that campaign. This is so we get the benefit of exporting them, or adding them to our Facebook custom audience.

Responsive Engagement Campaigns

These campaigns will help your system be more dynamic and user-responsive. I listed the *Fundamental System Campaigns* first, because I do believe them to be of higher priority. After you have them in place, however, start adding in these *Responsive Engagement Campaigns*, and you will further enhance your repeat business and email engagement.

5. The Birthday Campaign

Everyone likes gifts, and everyone likes to be remembered. A personalized Birthday campaign is a perfect way to do this. There is a free campaign available in the Infusionsoft Marketplace that works fairly well for this, though it does have a big limitation.

As I mentioned earlier in the book, a lot of people will have privacy concerns around the idea of giving you their full birthday. This is because it is a piece of personal data frequently used for identity theft. I know I personally will not give out my birthday to a marketing campaign. When I'm asked, I will usually just make up a date instead.

You can counteract this issue, however, by not asking for the full birthday. Instead, just ask for the birth month and day, or birth month and year. You can even ask for just their birth month.

Honestly, the birth month is all you really need to create a recurring marketing campaign that sends them some sort of gift or coupon code on the month of their birthday. I however, like to ask for either birth month AND birth day or birth year.

The reason is you then have a four-digit number. You can use a bit of marketing magic to get them to give it up to you. The way I do this is to give them some sort of free gift, but require them to login to get it. I tell them we set the default login password to their birth month and year as a four-digit number so they'll never forget it.

If you just ask them for just their birth month, it is a little tougher to get it, because they know it is for a marketing campaign. If, on the other hand, they think it is going to be used to unlock a gift, it is usually easier to get them to give you a four-digit code of MMDD or MMYY. As far as which of those two you should use, it really depends on your niche. The MMYY is the more desirable data to have, because it gives you some age demographics, but if your niche is particularly sensitive to privacy issues, you may want to go with MMDD instead.

6. The Anniversary Campaign

Now, before you object on privacy concerns, this is not the anniversary data you're thinking of. What I use this field for, instead, is to store the date when their account was first created. I then use that as an anniversary to celebrate with a little marketing flare.

When you send them an email with a subject of "Happy Anniversary! I really cherish you," "On this, our first anniversary, a gift for you," or something funny like that, it almost always gets opened. Then, you can reveal you're talking about the anniversary of when they first purchased from you, or first joined your list, or whatever other milestone you want to use. You can take the time to thank them for being a subscriber or customer, and reward them with some sort of freebie gift or promo code.

It is all about having an excuse to email them, and bring them back to your site to maybe buy something. It is also just an excuse to re-engage them, and create an opportunity to talk to them in a way very specific to them as an individual, so it feels personal and goodwill-based. Little things like this can go a long way towards maintaining happy subscribers and/or customers.

There is also some clever little logic used by the birthday campaign and this anniversary campaign. These are perpetual, or looping, campaigns. Once they finish, they restart themselves automatically. I recommend you download and install the free version of the Birthday Campaign from the Infusionsoft Marketplace, so you can look at the logic you'll need to use to make this work properly.

7. RFM and LCV Campaigns

RFM, or Recency-Frequency-Monetary, campaigns are vital, especially when combined with LCV (Lifetime Customer Value) data. I simply would not run any business without these core campaigns in place. These are, by far, the most popular campaigns that we sell. Please note, I have lumped them all together here for purposes of organization, but they are actually several different campaigns.

You'll have to use a third party app, such as MyFusion Helper (http://ismastery.com/free), or code up your own API extensions, to create and maintain these metrics. Not doing so, though, is really flying blind in your business. MyFusion Helper has a built-in function for updating the customer lifetime value data with a single HTTP POST widget in the Campaign Builder. While you can get this data from the default reports inside of Infusionsoft, you cannot automate around the data, because it has to be manually reported on.

What I do, instead, is store these critical metrics in custom fields on the contact record. That way, we can easily trigger automations around various situations. Let me give you some examples of when you might use this data.

The first thing I always recommend is having the data updated in real-time whenever any purchase is made by any contact. This way, after populating the data the first time, it will always be kept in sync, and update at all times. Also, there's no sense in updating it any other time, unless, perhaps, when you merge contacts.

The purchase data will stay stagnant, except when new purchases are made. So, this is the perfect time to update it. It is also super easy and convenient, since there are various triggers around purchase - with the Campaign Builder, E-Commerce actions, or Billing Automation - depending upon how you're configured.

One way you can create responsive engagement campaigns around this data is to check if the customer has crossed over certain thresholds every time a purchase is made. You can then automate accordingly by firing off other campaigns. For example, maybe on their first purchase, you want to give them a coupon code to encourage a second purchase, or, perhaps, when they've spent more than $500, you want to send them a handwritten letter to thank them for their business.

You can also use aging buckets to track the recency data. You add them into a campaign and begin a timer. At set intervals, you can perform actions accordingly, based upon, for example, age of last transaction. There are all kinds of options and possibilities here.

I recommend you do a little reading up on RFM methodologies, find a simple version that makes sense to you and implement it. As always, I recommend starting simple, but starting!

Here's an overview video all about RFM for you:

http://ismastery.com/rfm

8. Customer Satisfaction Survey Campaign (Automated Referral & Testimonial Generation)

So, this is a two-step process that involves, first, finding out the customers level of satisfaction via a quick survey or NPS (net promoter score) style survey. Then, based upon their responses, either reaching out to them to solve whatever issue they are not satisfied with, do nothing if they are content, but not obviously happy, or reach out for a testimonial or referral from the very happy clients. All of this would be automated, except the manual follow-up for unhappy customers.

Inexperienced marketers ask everyone for testimonials or referrals. Savvy marketers know a referral from a non-customer or poor customer is actually not a good thing. They also know, before they ask someone to leave a testimonial on an online site or forum, to first make sure the person is happy. It is best not to stir up a hornet's nest!

By making this a two-step process, we first determine if they're a good source or not. Then, we forward them on to the appropriate campaign. You can ask for either a referral or a testimonial, but it is my advice that you not ask for both. When you give people two choices, they are likely to do neither. Actually by including two options, you're presenting them with three - testimonial, referral or do nothing - and the latter will invariably be their response, because it will feel like you're asking for a lot.

The Best Practice is to ask for one or the other, and to mix up the campaigns so you can ask for both over time (if needed or part of your marketing approach).

9. Evergreen Quarterly Promotion Campaign

Short, somewhat aggressive promotions are good for a couple of reasons. Obviously, because they make money and give people a reason to buy, but, also, because if someone is going to unsub from your list just because you offer them a huge discount on a short promotion, that is a very non-engaged person, and you don't want them on your list anyway. So, having a quarterly promotion helps you to generate some additional revenue, as well as clean your list a little bit.

The promotion style I recommend is either a 48-hour flash sale or a 72-hour sale. Frank Kern likes to refer to this as a Four Day Cash Machine and has certainly popularized the promotion style. If you do the first option, you would email four times in three days. For example, if you start the promotion on Monday, you'd email on Monday, Tuesday and twice on Wednesday (once in the morning and once in the evening as a "last chance" offer before the promotion expires). If you were doing a 72-hour sale, you would just start one day sooner with an additional email.

I know many will argue that four emails in three days is a lot for your list - and it may be - but trust me, there is a reason for this. Before I tell you the reason, however, let's talk about how we structure the promotion. Then, we will come back to this common objection.

The first recommendation is you make it a digital promotion. That way, you can give them at least 50% off and some serious motivation to buy NOW. You do not want to make the mistake of just discounting 10%, or something like that. A ho-hum promotion is, in many cases, worse than no promotion at all, because you'll probably won't get much traction, and you'll still suffer higher than normal opt-outs.

By using a digital product as the offer, you can easily discount the price by 50% and not hurt your margins. If you don't have any digital products, then you'll have to get creative here. You may want to bundle some extra products with the sale, as well as offer free shipping and some percentage discount, as well. The point it, you really want to make it an irresistible offer.

Next, there is a psychology to how we approach the emails. Ideally, you need to add in a different, additional bonus, with each email you send out. So each day they're:

(a) Getting reminded of the huge savings

(b) Getting an added incentive (bonus) to purchase

(c) Realizing they are running out of time

These three psychological triggers work together to make this type of promotion very effective, as long as it is only used sparingly. You could, perhaps, run it every 60 or 75 days, but I recommend 90 days. If you run it too frequently, your list will get savvy to it and it will lose its effectiveness.

Lastly, the recommendation is that you make this an evergreen promotion - selling something you can sell year round, without any issue of seasonality. This way, you can very easily repurpose the promotion every 90-days without having to create it over from scratch. As a Best Practice, though, you may want to slightly revise it from promo to promo.

People love Flash Sales and buying at a discount. If you don't do it, they'll buy from someone else. It really has to be a compelling, truly irresistible offer, though, so they feel like they just can't pass it up. Also, it is good to tie it to some personal event, instead of some traditional marketing time of year.

As an example, I have done Flash Sales when I turned 40, when my son was born, and because my daughter got straight A's on her report card. All sorts of goofy reasons. People like to have a reason, and making it a personal one further solidifies your relationship and rapport with your list. It helps to personalize you more to your subscribers, and create a more powerful emotional bond.

Now, back to the objection that this promotion creates too many emails, too frequently. Yes, it is more aggressive than you probably would normally email your list, but that is a good thing. Every now and then, you need to purge your list from those that have a very weak level of commitment. If a contact is offended to the point of opting out of your list because of an occasional promotion designed to save them lots of money, well, it is best they get off your list anyway.

10. Free + Shipping Offer with 2 Upsells

This is one of those campaigns I truly feel almost every business should have actively running all of the time to attract new customers into their business. This campaign is better than a simple free report-style campaign with a traditional One Time Offer upsell.

With this campaign, you want to give something physical away FREE, but just charge them a minimal $4.95 shipping and handling fee. The purpose here is to build a buyers list - not just leads interested in freebies. You may lose a dollar or two on the front end offer, depending on what you give them and how much it costs to ship, but you should more than make up for that with your upsells and your back-end funnel.

The purpose of this funnel is to acquire buyer leads at a zero net sum cost. Meaning, with two 1-click upsells behind the Free + Shipping offer, even after ad spend costs, you should be at least breaking even. Having said that, it is not hard to make 3x ROI on these types of campaigns, provided they're done right, and the upsells are compelling.

This style of campaign will put buyers on your list, and buyers all share a very nice trend - they like to buy! That means, they'll not only buy some of your upsells on the Free + Shipping offer, but they'll likely be very good and responsive buyers on your list and backend products, as well.

There is no perfect funnel, so you'll have to experiment with what you offer on the Free + Shipping offer, as well as what prices you test for the Upsell #1 and Upsell #2 offers. Make sure they are true 1-click upsells, though. A 1-click upsell will not require them to re-enter their billing address or credit information, but simply confirm they want to add the item to their existing order. Once they do, it will instantly charge them.

Small, lightweight physical products, such as pen drives, CD's, DVD's, books, etc. make good Free + Shipping offers, but it will vary a lot by your market and/or niche. Likewise, the upsell prices will vary quite a bit by niche. In some niches, all you're trying to get is a simple $9.95 upsell. In other niches, though, anything less than $97 will be looked down upon.

You have to go with what you find works best in your niche, and you simply have to test it. Anyone who tells you something always works best at this price point or that price point, is someone you should run away from and not listen to. The fact is, offers vary widely in their effectiveness from niche to niche. In the end, all you can do is test.

Summary

This chapter is not meant to be, in any way, all-encompassing and comprehensive. Rather, it is meant to jumpstart you and get you thinking of how you could create more leveraged and responsive engagement-based automation marketing campaigns in your business to drive more engagement, more sales, and higher profits. Don't stop with these suggested campaigns. Instead, use them as a good starting point. Then, add to them over time with more of your own ideas and other examples of campaigns that you see working well.

CHAPTER 13

Summary

"Mastery is never truly achieved, only relentlessly pursued..."

Thank you for joining me on this journey towards Infusionsoft Mastery. By now, hopefully, you have come to think a little bit more like I do; that Mastery is never truly achieved, only relentlessly pursued.

The fact is, Infusionsoft will continue to evolve, as it has over the past several years I have been using it. My hope is you will evolve in your usage of Infusionsoft, as well, and this book, in some small part, can help shape that evolution to your betterment.

When I set out to write this book, I defined it more by what I didn't want the book to be, than what I did. In other words, I didn't want to create a simple, "how to" book, of which there are many already on the market. Instead, I wanted to address the critical components which shape the Best Practices approach I take with Infusionsoft personally, with all of my clients, and our SaaS company, as well. I wanted to give you the ability to really step beyond the technology, and into the higher-

level business understandings necessary to make that shift towards
Mastery.

At my core, I consider myself to be more of a businessman than a
marketer. I feel that, many times, the message gets lost in the cool whiz-
bang techno ramblings of this feature and that feature. At the end of the
day, though, Infusionsoft is a tool to grow your business. So, while
understanding the tech aspects are critical, understanding their
application to your business, and how to make it grow, is what really
matters.

As I've said several times in this book, Marketing Automation is
merely the grease between the gears of your business. It makes your
business run smoother, faster, and with less friction to keep the gears of
business moving. However, whether they're moving your business
towards rapid growth and success, or rapidly accelerating your demise, is
much less about the technology, and much more about your business.

My goal is for this book to become a long-term reference for you.
One that you read over and over again – even if just chapter by chapter –
as you proceed along your path towards Infusionsoft mastery in your
business. The core concepts and principles of this book were intended to
be timeless. Well, as timeless as possible. It is next to impossible to truly
write a timeless technology book, and I'm sure other updates and
revisions will follow.

If you've reached this point, and are asking yourself, "where do I
start?" I would encourage you to go back to Chapter 2 – Core Concepts,
where I talk about The Five Stages of Infusionsoft Mastery. Spend a little
time just assessing where you truly are on your path towards mastery,
and what you can do to take just one more step down that pathway.

Mastery doesn't happen overnight, and as much as I'd love to be able
to certify you as Infusionsoft Masters now, reading a book on the topic

will hardly transform you in one fell swoop. Don't even worry about that, though. Just focus on the next step.

Those Five Stages of Infusionsoft Mastery really do exist. They serve as a checkpoint to where you are, and how much farther you can go. Not everyone will progress through all five stages. That's fine, but to truly get the most out of the large software investment you've already made, or are considering making with Infusionsoft, all five stages are the natural progression.

The culmination of that process for me lead to the creation of our SaaS company, to further expand the envelope of what was possible with Infusionsoft. Our MyFusion Helper app continues to grow in features, month after month, as we continue to evolve. To try it out yourself at no risk via our free trial, you can go to:

http://ismastery.com/free

We will always strive to meet the increasing needs of sophisticated marketers and businessmen and women all over the globe, seeking to improve their business and, indirectly, their lives, via Infusionsoft marketing automation.

I invite you to continue this journey with me by going to the link below to access the additional Bonus Material for this book:

http://ismastery.com/bonus

Doing so will allow you to stay in the conversation we've started here, as well as keep up to date with our blog, tools and resources.

Lastly, I leave you with this final reminder. Treat everything you do in Infusionsoft, and your business, as an experiment. Don't let yourself think shortsightedly on just, "this campaign," or "this marketing sequence." Instead, always find ways to interject small tests into everything you do. The key to rapid improvement and growth is learning how to fail forward fast. You can only do that by learning, and you can only learn by trying, testing and tracking.

Remember, the ultimate goal of Marketing Automation is to fuel and propel your business so it feeds the lifestyle you wish to create. For me, that means leverage and location independence. With my international family and multiple homes on the West Coast, East Coast and in Brasil, everything I can do with Marketing Automation to streamline my business, I do.

I know this is a technical business and financial book, but, honestly, money is not really what drives or motivates me. To me, it is about the lifestyle technology can provide. I am grateful for the technology advances Infusionsoft extends to my business, but I am much more motivated by the freedom and flexibility it provides for my life and my family.

For example, for the past six-months, I have travelled around the entire Western portion of the country with my family and lived on the road. It was not a vacation, though we saw many vacation destinations.

I bought a large RV and we lived on the road. I ran all three of my businesses from the road and spent months showing my children around the country – an experience we all loved. Freedom is what drives me. Marketing automation is simply an enabler.

My sincere goal of this book is not to convert you into an RV driving road warrior – unless that is your dream – but rather to help you achieve the goals you have for you and your family, beyond just making money.

To your success,

Troy Broussard

The Missing Chapter

Online Bonus Material

Why a "missing" chapter?

Despite my best efforts, I know the moment this book goes to print, it will already begin to age. Technology, unlike a good wine, doesn't get better with age (unfortunately). That's why I knew providing additional online supplemental content was a must!

Infusionsoft is also a technology product that really benefits from screen capture and screen cast video, as well. It is one thing to read about how to do something. It is entirely different to see it live, on a step-by-step video that really shows you exactly what to do. That level of content simply can't be provided via a book.

So, I decided to make additional content available for free to all book owners. There is no cost or catch. You simply need to go to the following link to gain access to your additional content and trainings:

http://ismastery.com/bonus

Inside this private members area, you'll find additional information, updates, resources, video training and more.

But I wanted to go one step further and give you that extra kick in the pants to get things moving with your own Infusionsoft mastery. I know learning is one thing, but sometimes just rolling up your sleeves and doing something goes a lot further.

So, I've decided to provide you with one of my Foundation Series campaigns <u>absolutely free</u>! Inside the members area, you'll find a request form where you can ask for the campaign to be installed directly into your own Infusionsoft app – no charge!

What's the campaign?

I thought long and hard on which campaign to provide you. At the end of the day, I decided on my Email Engagement Tracking Campaign, because I know it has 100% broad appeal to everyone, and also addresses the most fundamental need of every email marketer – keeping your list warm and engaged!

This campaign uses only Infusionsoft data for tracking email opens and clicks, so you don't have to worry about any interpreted data errors. The campaign will tell you who is engaged on your list, who isn't, who has never opened or clicked on an email (ever), and also will age their engagement in 30, 60, 90, 120, 150 and 180 buckets!

These buckets allow you to create automatic trigger points where, if someone hasn't engaged with you in 30 days, for example, you can automatically launch them into a marketing campaign offering them something really cool to get their attention and bring them back into the fold before they go cold. You can do this in any of the buckets, creating unlimited flexibility – all 100% automated.

This campaign is part of our Foundation series of campaigns for a reason; it is one of the most important campaigns I install on all of my private clients.

The members area is not a stagnant area. Over time, I will provide additional updates and resources as the tides of technology shift, and I can help you keep up with the latest trends and marketing tactics.

Enjoy!

Made in the USA
Charleston, SC
20 January 2017